KT-392-221

Egypt

An Illustrated History

BROMLEY PUBLIC LIBRARIES	
02431250**9**	
H J	14/05/2002
962	£11.50
ORP.APB *BEC*	

Fred James Hill

HIPPOCRENE BOOKS, INC.

NEW YORK

BROMLEY LIBRARIES

3 0128 02431 2509

IMAGE CREDITS

Photos by:
Christina Joyce 10, 15, 29, 44, 133
Kevin Smith 9, 11, 66, 67 (left & right),
87, 77, 101, 148
Egyptian State Tourist Office, London 8, 31, 40,
42, 43, 51, 72 (above & below), 150
Teresa Machan 12

Woodcuts on pages 83, 87, 97 by E.W. Lane,
taken from his book *Manners and Customs of
the Modern Egyptians* (1836)

Illustrations on pages 21, 27, 33, 53 taken
from E.A. Wallis Budge's *Dwellers on the Nile*
& those on pages 25, 37 from his *Egyptian
Ideas of the Afterlife* 25, 37

All maps & tables by Fred Hill

Copyright © 2001 by Fred J. Hill

All rights reserved.

Typeset & designed by Fred Hill/Desert♥Hearts

ISBN 0-7818-0911-8

For information, address:
HIPPOCRENE BOOKS, INC.
171 Madison Avenue
New York, NY 10016

www.hippocrenebooks.com

Printed in the United States of America.

Contents

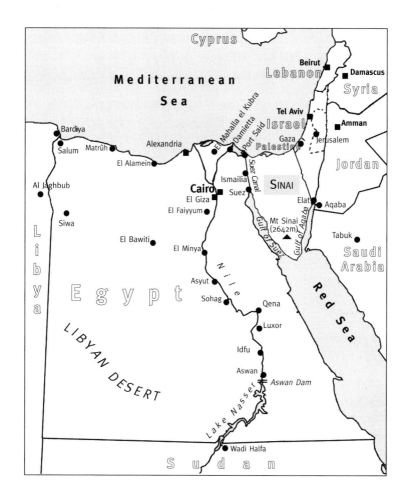

Modern Egypt and the Middle East.

INTRODUCTION

K nown to the Egyptians by its ancient Semitic name *Misr*, modern Egypt is amongst the largest of the Arabic republics. Its heart is overcrowded Cairo, a modern city crammed with crumbling desert-beaten buildings and chaotic traffic-choked streets. It is a place filled with the unexpected, where each corner holds the promise of a new surprise as the modern brushes shoulders with a far older way of life. Ancient mosques and dusty high-rise apartments compete with each other as street vendors jostle for space in their shade. Markets, hidden down ancient narrow alleyways, are often given away only by the fragrant, musty smells of spices that are sold in abundance from overflowing open sacks, much as they have been for many centuries.

The country has long captured the world's imagination as the magical land of the Pharaohs and their awe-inspiring Pyramids of Giza—the only one of the Seven Wonders of the Ancient World to survive. Home to one of the greatest civilizations in history, spanning a period of some 3,000 years, pharaonic Egypt offers us a wonderful glimpse into the lives of our forebears, whose highly developed and sophisticated culture has lost none of its power to impress and surprise.

Yet the history of Egypt since that time is no less fascinating or significant, especially given the nation's role in the development of world religion. The Egyptians were among the earliest peoples to adopt the Christian faith, and its deserts provided fertile ground for

The Sphinx and Great Pyramid—two of the world's greatest monuments.

the development of monasticism, a tradition that spread beyond the frontiers of Egypt to reach the world at large.

Islam arrived with the Arab conquests of the 7th century and the country subsequently went on to become a major cultural and spiritual heart of the Muslim world. Its most famous landmark, the al-Azhar Mosque in Cairo, founded in the 10th century, has long been a source of great pride for Muslims. In keeping with a country that is no stranger to longevity, al-Azhar's prestigious teaching institution, which attracts scholars from around the world, is considered to be the oldest university in existence.

Today the overwhelming majority of the country's approximately 65 million inhabitants are Muslim. City horizons are dotted with the minarets of mosques and, every day, their speakers crackle with

Ancient and modern standing side-by-side in the city of Cairo.

the evocative, almost ethereal, calls of the *muezzins* summoning the faithful to prayer. On Fridays, the special day of prayer, mosques are filled to bursting point and sidewalks and prayer mats spill out onto the sidewalks and streets.

Yet the population is not uniformly Muslim. Christianity continues to thrive in Egypt, and a significant minority of the country belongs to the distinctive Egyptian church whose members are known as Copts. The country is also home to a million or so Christians of other denominations, such as the Roman Catholic Church, and the Greek and Armenian Orthodox Churches. For many centuries Egypt was also home to a flourishing community of Jews, though most left the country after the creation of the state of Israel in 1948. Today only a handful remain in Cairo.

Political and Social Life

The heart of social life in Egypt can be found in the innumerable cafes where the latest news is discussed over a tea and a *shisha*, a

A bustling street in Cairo.

tall waterpipe used to smoke tobacco. As often as not, the topic will touch upon recent developments in politics and the government's latest progress, if any, in attempting to address the number of serious issues that concern the country: overpopulation, corruption, low salaries, housing shortages and general poverty.

Although the country has a multi-party system, democracy is somewhat theoretical rather than real. Opposition parties have found the going tough, and few have succeeded in winning more than a token number of seats in the elected parliament.

Political life is dominated by the pro-government National Democratic Party (NDP), and the exceptionally strong hand of the president, whose term lasts six years but is renewable by popular referendum. In fact, from the time of the Republic's inception in 1952 to the end of the century, there were only four presidents—Naguib, Nasser, Sadat, and Mubarak—all highly distinguished military officers, and none readily given to criticism. That is not to Egypt's leaders have been unpopular. On the contrary, despite occasionally incurring the displeasure or even wrath of certain groups or factions, they frequently receive immense support from the population.

The head of the government is the presidentially-appointed prime minister. Egypt's parliament has two chambers: the People's Assembly, which is the legislative body, and the Consultative Council, which has advisory powers only. Ten members of the People's Assembly are appointed by the president, while 454 are elected to five-year terms by popular

Minarets reaching into the Cairene sky.

vote. In the case of the Consultative Council, 88 are appointed by the president and 176 are elected by the people. Heading each of the country's 26 administrative units is an appointed governor.

A constitutional ban against religious-based parties reflects the very real threat posed to national security by Islamic fundamentalist movements. Many of these extremist groups gained a great deal of popularity in response to the historical lack of outlets for political and social grievances. Some are responsible for a number of assassinations and terrorist attacks that have rocked the country in the recent past. In a vicious circle, acts such as these have seriously hampered attempts to introduce more political freedom.

Despite this, Egypt remains amongst the more tolerant and forward-looking of the Arabic countries and is one of the most influential. Its diplomatic service is the largest in the Arab world and is highly active in the international arena, producing figures such as United Nations Secretary General Boutros Boutros Ghali. Egypt has also enjoyed a special place in the world of Arabic culture, leading the way in music, films, television, literature and

An Egyptian with his camels in Sinai.

the press. The distinctive Egyptian dialect is understood around the Arabic-speaking world and is usually the form chosen by those wishing to learn colloquial Arabic, since it is the most accessible to foreign students and visitors.

No stranger to tourism—the Englishman Thomas Cooke first began to organize package holidays as early as the 1860s—Egypt has long welcomed visitors and works hard to protect its national heritage. There are of course huge financial rewards, and the tourist sector plays a vital part in the Egyptian economy, being the country's second largest source of revenue after remittances from expatriate workers. Visitors are not only attracted by the country's astounding cultural heritage but also by the natural beauty of the Nile and the coastline of the Red Sea.

The 9th-century Mosque of Ibn Tulun, in Cairo—one of the earliest and most famous examples of Egyptian Islamic architecture.

Egypt—The Gift of the Nile

To borrow a phrase from Herodotus, a Greek historian who traveled widely during the 5th century B.C., Egypt was no less than a "Gift of the Nile." Water is still a highly valued commodity in a country that is just over three times the size of the state of New Mexico, and is more than 90 percent desert. With temperatures that reach as high as 110°F in the summer and no significant rainfall throughout the year, survival depends on the Nile River. It is here in the fertile valley and delta regions, that the overwhelming majority of the Egyptian population lives—an area of land that makes up as little as four percent of the entire country.

Like a huge artery, the world's longest river, stretching 4,150 miles from its source to the sea, courses through the entire length of Egypt, pumping water and nutrients into its immediate surroundings before flowing out into the Mediterranean Sea. Away from the Nile and oasis towns there are few signs of human or animal life.

For thousands of years, the Nile has served also as a highway along which boats have sailed up and down laden with cargo, including rocks from quarries destined to be used in the making of pyramids and other monuments. This travel is made considerably easier by prevailing winds, which run counter to the flow of the river. Thus, sailors have been able to use the current to carry their boats down the Nile and their sails to carry them up. Boats called *feluccas*, with their distinctive lateen sails, can still be seen plying the waters of the Nile—an evocative sight that would surely be appreciated by the ancient Egyptians were they here today.

Introduction

Feluccas sailing on the waters of the Nile at Luxor.

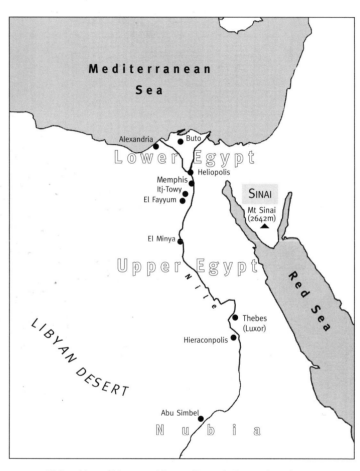

Major cities of Upper and Lower Egypt during ancient times.

THE AGE OF THE PHARAOHS

Many thousands of years ago, Egypt was inhabited by nomadic tribes who foraged for food in the rich vegetation of the banks of the Nile, and who hunted the many wild animals that once thrived on the savannah plains that covered the region. Climatic changes led to a process of desertification, and, in time, groups began to settle permanently along the waters of the river. By around 4000 B.C., the Nile Valley and Delta were teeming with sedentary agricultural communities that had come to live in harmony with the river, waiting for the annual floods before planting their crops in the rich soil that lined its banks.

In time, these flourishing settlements, which originally had little mutual contact, began to establish strong links with each other. The newly-forged bonds gave rise to the creation of two kingdoms—that of Lower Egypt, in the Nile Delta, with its capital at Buto, and that of Upper Egypt in the south, with its capital at Hieraconpolis.

In approximately 3100 B.C., an event occured that would profoundly affect the future of the region. It was then that a powerful king by the name of Menes, the ruler of Upper Egypt, launched a military campaign and united the two kingdoms. King Menes subsequently established his capital at Memphis, which sat at the point where the Nile Valley meets the Delta, some 15 miles south of present-day Cairo. The unification of Egypt laid the foundations of a single state and gave birth to a new era—that of the pharaohs.

The Old Kingdom

The pharaohs of Egypt ruled over one of the oldest and most spectacular civilizations in the world, spanning an astonishing period of more than 3,000 years. During this time a succession of 31 dynasties ruled the land, beginning with Menes himself in 3100 B.C. and ending with the last Egyptian pharaoh Nectanebo II in 343 B.C.

It is customary to break this surprisingly lengthy period of ancient Egyptian history into three so-called "Kingdoms"—the Old, Middle, and the New—each of which enjoyed more or less sustained political and social stability. However, each of these periods was followed by an era of crippling instability and war, as the central government lost its grip over the country and the union fell into disrepair. These difficult times are referred to collectively as the three "Intermediate" periods.

The first few hundred years after Menes' unification of Egypt were vital in the development of the country's social, political and economic life. During this time, the first two ruling dynasties strengthened the unification of the country and laid the foundations of the system of central government that would last throughout the pharaonic era. Once a sufficient degree of stability was finally achieved, the country's political and cultural life blossomed under the 3rd and 4th dynasties, and it was then that the Old Kingdom began in earnest. It was to prove an astonishingly productive period that saw, amongst other achievements, the construction of the awe-inspiring pyramids as well as major developments in religion and the art of writing hieroglyphs.

The king, who from around 2500 B.C. onwards was believed to be the son of the sun-god Ra, was the all-powerful ruler over the land and considered to be a direct link between his subjects and the gods. He bore the title of "King of Upper and Lower Egypt" and "Lord of the Two Lands," and wore two crowns that symbolized the union of the two realms.

Heading the military, legal and religious institutions of the state, the pharaoh was charged with the critical task of

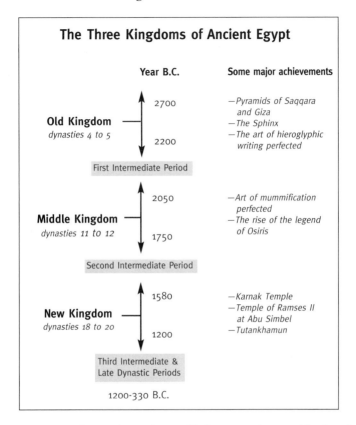

The Three Kingdoms of Ancient Egypt

	Year B.C.	Some major achievements
Old Kingdom dynasties 4 to 5	2700 2200	—Pyramids of Saqqara and Giza —The Sphinx —The art of hieroglyphic writing perfected
First Intermediate Period		
Middle Kingdom dynasties 11 to 12	2050 1750	—Art of mummification perfected —The rise of the legend of Osiris
Second Intermediate Period		
New Kingdom dynasties 18 to 20	1580 1200	—Karnak Temple —Temple of Ramses II at Abu Simbel —Tutankhamun
Third Intermediate & Late Dynastic Periods		

1200-330 B.C.

maintaining order and warding off chaos in the world, thereby ensuring the continued support of the gods. Such was the awe in which the ruler was held, it was reported that during the 5th Dynasty a courtier by the name of Washptah was so overcome after kissing the feet of his pharaoh Neferirkare that he died—normally subjects were restricted to merely kissing the ground on which their king walked.

The term "pharaoh," in fact, only came to be used to refer to the king much later on during the New Kingdom. The word derived from *Per Ao*, meaning "The Great House"—the name given to the administration complex surrounding the royal court at Memphis.

Egyptian society was highly stratified. At the top of the complex social ladder were those who derived their authoriy from the pharaoh, starting with the vizier (chief minister), whose job it was to maintain law and order, and to oversee major architectural projects. Beneath him were numerous high-ranking government officials and high priests, followed by the lesser officials, priests, bureaucrats and land owners. At the bottom were the mass of laborers and peasants.

A vast bureaucracy was needed to ensure the smooth running of the state, and this in turn depended on a highly sophisticated system of taxation from which there were few exemptions. Taxes were collected in kind, and the produce stored in granaries. Building projects would often require large numbers of mouths to feed, and it was vital to keep the granaries well stocked if work was to be completed.

By all accounts, women did not fare too badly in ancient Egypt, at least insofar as the law was concerned. They were entitled to inherit, buy, and sell property and enjoyed the same rights as men. However, that is not to say that there were not very real social distinctions that excluded women from various kinds of activities and opportunities.

The Land of Plenty

Writing about the Nile Delta, Herodotus claimed to have known no other land that was as easy to farm. The key to the fertility of the Nile Delta and Valley was the annual flooding (as a result of tropical rains in the Ethiopian tableland), bringing in its wake

Irrigating the fields—an ancient Egyptian drawing
water from the Nile using a *shaduf*, a leather
bucket attached to a long pivoted pole.

deposits of thick black mud that nourished the surrounding lands
with rich minerals. It was for this reason that the Egyptians called
the Nile Valley *Kemet*—the "Black Land." With the aid of
comprehensive networks of irrigation channels, the Egyptians were
able to maximize the benefits of the floods. The flooding season
was between July and October. By March the following year, the
crops would be ready to harvest. Crop yields were intricately linked
to the height of the water, and taxes levied by the state were
adjusted annually to take the level of flooding into account.

Once intensive agriculture had become highly developed along
the Nile Valley, interaction between the permanent settlers and
those who lived out in the desert regions all but ceased. Indeed,
the river dwellers came to view the desert, known as *deshet*,
meaning "Red Land," in a negative light and to develop a distrust
of the nomadic tribes that roamed it.

Wheat and barley were the two principal crops grown in pharaonic Egypt. Other favorite crops were lentils, cucumbers, onions, leeks, garlic, figs and grapes. Flax was grown and used to make linen; while papyrus, which grew in abundance in ancient Egypt, was used to make writing paper—the first of its kind—as well as rope, mats and even small rafts. However, the country's lack of forests meant that wood was at a premium, and had to be imported from the far-off region of Lebanon.

The key staple of the ancient Egyptians was bread, which was made into cakes and loaves of varying shapes. They were also partial to beer and produced this from various kinds of grain that were fashioned into cakes, broken up and then fermented. It was not only a drink to be enjoyed by the living—it was also one of the most important drinks used in ritual offerings to the dead. Nor was it the only alchoholic drink enjoyed by the population—wine made from grapes was similarly consumed by the richer sections of society.

The ancient Egyptians were no strangers to drunken behavior, and it was clearly frowned upon by some, as demonstrated in a contemporary letter in which a teacher admonishes a young scribe. In it he complains: "I know you frequently abandon your studies and whirl around in pleasure, that you wander from street to street, and every house stinks of beer when you leave it. . . If only you would realize that alcohol is a curse, you would put wine aside, and leave beer alone."

Domesticated animals played an important part in Egypt. Cattle were kept for their milk, another favorite drink of ancient Egyptians, as well as for their ability to pull wooden plows in the fields. Other domestic animals included sheep, goats and ducks, as well as cats and hunting dogs. Donkeys were also valued as beasts of burden, but Egypt had to wait until 1600 B.C. before horses arrived from Asia. Camels, which have become closely identified with Egypt, were introduced much later by the Persians who invaded in the 6th century B.C.

The ancient Egyptians were also skilled in the art of bee-keeping and the abundance of flowers along the Nile provided excellent conditions for them to produce honey. The honey and wax collected was used in a variety of products—mead, medicines, amulets, and figures for religious ceremonies—as well as in the process of embalming the dead.

Religion in Ancient Egypt

Religion played a central role in the lives of the ancient Egyptians. The inhabitants of the region had long worshiped natural objects such as animals, stones, trees, and mountains. Over a period of time, a colorful pantheon of animal gods emerged—a reflection of the varied wildlife that once thrived in Egypt. Although these gods were initially represented in their natural forms, many were eventually depicted in human form, with only the heads retaining animal features. Amongst these animal deities were the lion-god Mahes, the hippopotamus-goddess Taurit, the crocodile-god Sebek, and the frog-goddess Heqit.

The scarab beetle was also sacred, and the most popular of good-luck charms. On account of its habit of pushing a ball of dung over large distances, the beetle came to be identified with the sun-god Khapre, who in Egyptian mythology pushed the sun across the sky everyday. Furthermore, the scarab's young, which seemed to miraculously hatch from dung, was likened to life emerging from the earth, thereby making the beetle a powerful symbol of regeneration. Accordingly, it was customary to bury scarab-shaped amulets with the dead.

The cat was also accorded a special place in Egyptian society. The cat-headed goddess Bastet was closely identified with the

Major Gods in the Ancient Egyptian World

Khnemu, the
great builder of
the universe.

Ptah, creator-god of
Memphis and patron
god of craftsmen.

Anubis, god of the
dead and patron
god of embalmers.

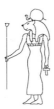

Sekhmet, the lion-headed
goddess associated with
negative forces of the sun.

Mut, the mother
goddess of Thebes,
and wife of Amun-Ra.

Bastet, cat-goddess
associated with the
power of the sun.

Thoth, the scribe of
the gods.

Khonsu, the
moon-god.

Ra, the sun-god
of Heliopolis.

Horus, falcon-headed god of the sky (latterly known as son of Osiris and Isis.)

Amun, great god of Thebes.

Osiris, god of the afterworld and fertility.

Isis suckling her son, Horus. Wife of Osiris, she was the great mother goddess.

Ancient Egyptian design featuring the scarab beetle, closely identified with the sun-god Khephre.

sun's power to ripen crops. The reverence in which cats were held led the Egyptians to develop something of a penchant for embalming their feline friends, as testified to by the countless cat-mummies discovered lying in special cemeteries.

The abundance of different gods did not mean that Egyptians worshipped them all. In fact each village had its own deity, one that might well be completely unknown by outsiders. Usually, these gods were presented as triads, that is with their wife and child. In the case of the big-city gods, their status very much depended on the fortunes of their city. Thus when a city became the capital, its principal deity would be elevated to the status of the national god. For example, when Memphis was the capital, its god Ptah was the national god. When Thebes became the capital, the god Amun was similarly brought to prominence. These the national gods were, by and large, the concern of the ruling elite. They played little or no part in the lives of ordinary Egyptians, who continued to worship local gods in temples especially dedicated to them.

In ancient Egyptian mythology, the gods were, in fact, believed to have originally been mortals, albeit ones who were extraordinary and extremely long-lived. Having died, it was the job of the temple priests to ensure that their spirit, known as the *ka*, was perpetuated. Therefore, in temples that were often erected on the site where the god in question was thought to have been buried, the priests summoned the *ka* daily, using pictures or statues, and made vital offerings food and drink to ensure their eternal survival.

Mummies—The Art of Preservation

Pharaohs and wealthy Egyptians were extremely concerned over the fate of their own spirits. In order to ensure that their souls survived into the afterlife, they adopted the unusual practice of having their bodies mummified. They believed that once the soul had survived the tests of the underworld, it was vital for it to rejoin its body each morning. Therefore, preserving the body against decay was necessary if the soul was to recognize and reuse it.

Mummies got their name by accident. In medieval times, physicians believed that bitumen had near miraculous healing powers that could used to treat disorders ranging from cuts to tuberculosis. It was mistakenly thought that

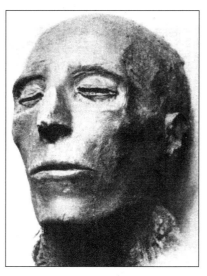

The mummified head of Pharaoh Seti I, ruler of Egypt around 1320 B.C.

the black coating found on mummies was also *mumia*, meaning "bitumen" in Arabic. As a result, mummies became highly prized for their supposed medicinal properties. The truth was, however, that the blackness was merely a chemical reaction between the various substances used in the embalming process.

The practice of mummification was developed soon after the construction of the first pyramids, and fully perfected during the New Kingdom—although more primitive attempts to preserve the body, without the use of chemicals, had been attempted prior to this. Preparing the body for burial took 70 days altogether. The embalmer began by making an incision on the left side of the abdomen in order to remove the internal organs, most of which were then placed in special stone canopic jars to protect them from spells being cast against the deceased. There they remained, until needed by the dead person. The brain was usually removed by scooping it out through a hole made at the back the nose, and then discarded.

The body was dried out by packing it in crystals of natron, a kind of salt, and leaving it for 40 days, after which the cavity was padded with linen and sawdust and false eyes placed in the sockets. The embalmers then rubbed in oils and plant resins to soften the skin. Next, the body was swathed in bandages between which special charms were inserted. Over the face a painted mask was placed, which in the case of royalty would be made of gold. Finally it was placed in a coffin of wood or stone. Many examples of wooden coffins have survived until the present, with their sides elaborately painted with hieroglyphs and representations of objects needed for the afterlife, such as beer and bread. Along with the four canopic jars, the coffin was handed over to priests for burial. In the case of a pharaoh, the tomb would often be spectacular.

The Pyramids

The desire for eternity was also the driving force behind the construction of the pyramids, the sheer scale and technological mastery of which continues to be a source of wonder. Built as tombs for kings and sometimes queens, these world-famous monuments did not stand in isolation, but were designed as part of funerary complexes that included shrines and temples, where priests would summon the spirits of the royalty and make offerings to ensure their immortality. Between 2700 and 1640 B.C., a great number of pyramids were constructed and, although many have since been reduced to rubble, dozens of examples still survive today.

The first master pyramid-builder was an architect by the name of Imhotep. Around 2680 B.C., he was commissioned to build a

The Step Pyramid at Saqqara, the oldest hewn stone monument in Egypt.

tomb for the pharaoh Zoser, and, as was customary, work commenced during the monarch's lifetime. Imhotep started by building a tomb in the form of a traditional *mastaba*. These were long flat rectangular buildings, built of sun-baked mud bricks, with walls standing around 12 feet high. The name *mastaba* derives from the Arabic "bench," on account of the tomb's similarity to a long stone seat typically found outside Egyptian homes in later times. The innovative Imhotep, however, used stone as his medium and continued to add to the tomb until he had created a six-layered, stepped pyramid, standing 200 feet high. The result was the Step Pyramid at Saqqara, the first monument in Egypt to be made entirely out of hewn stone.

The Pyramids at Giza—from left to right: Mycerinus, Khafre, and Khufu. (The limestone casing which gave the pyramids smooth faces can still be seen at the top of Khafre.)

The vast expense and labor involved in its construction is a clear demonstration of the considerable power exercised by the Egyptian kings. Imhotep, who also appears to have been a scholar and physician, was held in such great respect that he was worshipped as a god after his death. His superb achievement still stands today at the ancient site of Memphis, south of Cairo.

By the fourth dynasty (approximately 2600 B.C. to 2500 B.C.), the Egyptians had perfected their phenomenal architectural skills, enabling them to construct the most spectacular and famous of all the Pyramids—those at Giza.

Unlike the Step Pyramid, these pyramids—known as Khufu, Khafre and Mycerinus—were of true pyramidal form and were originally constructed with smooth white limestone faces. Such was the wonder they inspired that they were considered to be one of the Seven Wonders of the Ancient World.

The largest of the Pyramids at Giza, named after and built for the pharaoh Khufu, who ruled between 2589 B.C. and 2566 B.C.,

The Sphinx, set against the backdrop of the Pyramids at Giza.

stands 481 feet high. Its construction was an immensely costly business, involving many thousands of skilled workers (not slaves) over a period of some 20 years. The monument contains around two and a half million blocks of stone, whose average weight is more than two and a half tons, with some weighing as much as fifteen. Most of the stone used was locally quarried limestone. Granite, a much harder stone, was also used for the construction of the burial chambers and internal passages. This was brought by river a distance of more than 500 miles from quarries in Aswan in the south. The stones were then dragged into place by means of ramps.

Standing next to Khufu are the later pyramids of Khafre (471 feet high) and Mycerinus (204 feet). The Khafre funerary complex is also home to the famous limestone statue of the Sphinx, the oldest and largest of the many images of man-headed lions.

Dwarfed by the colossal pyramids, the Sphinx is, nevertheless, a huge monument, standing 66 feet high and 240 feet long.

The statue, whose head is thought to be that of the pharaoh Khafre himself, was intended to represent a divine guardian. Between its paws is an inscribed granite slab which describes a dream that a prince named Tuthmosis had while resting in its shade during a gazelle hunt. He dreamed that he was approached by the Sphinx, who promised him the kingdom if he cleared the sand that covered his body and that was making breathing difficult. Tuthmosis obliged the Sphinx and went one step further, ordering the construction of mud-brick walls around the monument to prevent further encroachment. That the Sphinx was good to his word is demonstrated by the 3000-year-old slab placed by Tuthmosis IV, the new pharaoh of the land.

Hieroglyphs—Divine Writing

Like the Pyramids and the Sphinx, ancient Egyptian hieroglyphs rank amongst the most famous images in the world. These evocative symbols first appeared around 3100 B.C. and would be used to adorn monuments until the time of the Roman Empire. Knowledge of hieroglyphic writing died out shortly thereafter, however, and the script would remain inaccessible for some 1,400 years.

The breakthrough came in 1799, when a French soldier in Napolean's campaign chanced upon a damaged black basalt stone during the construction of a fort at Raschid, near the mouth of the of the Rosetta branch of the Nile Delta. Etched on the stone was a decree of 196 B.C., written by priests to honor the ruling pharaoh, Ptolemy Epiphanes. It featured three identical texts—two in Egyptian and one in Greek (the official language of Egypt at the time).

The top section featured hieroglyphic text; the middle section was in demotic, a later simplified version of hieroglyphs that could be written with greater speed and ease; and the bottom section was written in the Greek alphabet.

Back in Europe, Egyptologists had little problem translating the Greek, but the pictorial nature of the hieroglyphs confused them. It was the Frenchman Jean François Champollion who finally realized that some of the signs made up an alphabet and represented sounds rather than things. His discovery allowed scholars to put together a grammar of the Egyptian language and decipher the ancient text in 1822.

Hieroglyphs did, in fact, begin as pictorial representations of actual objects that could be understood by anyone familiar with them, but they were highly restrictive in that they could not express abstract ideas. To address this problem, 24 hieroglyphs were set aside

The Rosetta Stone, featuring the three texts used by Egyptologists to decipher the mysterious hieroglyphs. (It is now displayed in the British Museum.)

to represent the sounds of the Egyptian language. In addition to these, hundreds of other hieroglyphs were retained in their original pictorial form to complement the phonetic symbols. This combination made hieroglyphic writing extremely complex—an art form of which the Egyptians were justifiably proud. In fact, they considered it no less than a divine gift of Thoth, the god of wisdom and learning.

Only those in the highest reaches of society, such as members of the royal family and key officials, were taught to read and write. Scribes themselves enjoyed a special status in society, a fact illustrated by the following text written on an ancient piece of papyrus which declared: "The scribe directs every work in the land. . . he pays no taxes. . . his tribute is paid in writing."

Some hieroglyphs were considered extremely sacred. The ankh, which was originally a hieroglyph representing a sandal with a loop, was especially powerful, coming to symbolize eternal life and widely used as an amulet.

The sacred ankh, a symbol of eternal life.

The Middle Kingdom

After a succession of wonderfully productive centuries, Egypt faltered at some point during the sixth dynasty and entered a bleak phase of its history know as the First Intermediate Period, lasting approximately 150 years. Although the exact reasons for the decline remain unknown, the country suffered a number of upheavals: power struggles amongst powerful governors, poor harvests, famine and poverty. Moreover, increasing decentralization led to the collapse of the monarchy and to civil war. Although there was a succession of dynasties during this time, they exercised only limited and local control. It was the powerful eleventh dynasty, the Mentuhoteps, based in Thebes, who managed to seize control of the country around 1280 B.C. and bring order back to the land.

Making Hieroglyphic Words

An example of how the Egyptians wrote *apt*, their word for "duck":

 represents the sound A

 represents the sound P

 represents the sound T

 represents the idea of a duck itself, not a sound

Therefore, once put together, "duck" written in hieroglyphs would be:

United once again, Egypt experienced a lengthy period of peace and economic prosperity. The country was initially ruled from Thebes, but the capital was later moved to Itj-Towy, located in the region of Fayyum, about 60 miles southwest of modern Cairo. The area was originally a large marshy depression into which the Nile waters overflowed during the annual inundation. Under the 12th-dynasty pharaoh Amenemhet I (*r.* 1991-1962 B.C.) the Egyptians turned the depression into a permanent lake, bringing about an agricultural transformation of the region.

In addition to maintaining its trading partnership with Lebanon in order to ensure steady supplies of valuable wood, extensive trading links were also developed with the people of Nubia to the far south, from whom the Egyptians obtained granite and gold.

The Legend of Osiris—Eternal Life for All

The Middle Kingdom also saw a new trend in religious belief. Egyptians were deeply preoccupied by the question of life after death, and one myth seems to have struck a profound chord in them—that of Osiris. Both god and man, Osiris suffered a terrible death, but his subsequent resurrection held the promise of eternal life for the ordinary Egyptian, a reward previously thought to be out of the reach of all except the rich and powerful.

According to the myth, Osiris was a much-loved Egyptian king who urged his countrymen to give up their barbarous ways and live good lives in accordance with the laws of the land and of the gods. Yet, Osiris had a great enemy in the person of his jealous brother Seth, who set about plotting his destruction. Seth secretly had a beautiful golden chest made to fit the exact specifications of Osiris's body and then organized a banquet to which he invited the unsuspecting king. There, he asked his guests to try the chest out for size, offering to give it to whomever it fit. One by one the guests climbed in, but predictably it matched no one. Until Osiris's turn, that is. Seth's men immediately sealed the chest and threw it in the Nile, where it was carried off downstream.

Grief-stricken, Osiris's wife and sister, Isis, went in search of her unfortunate husband's body, which she eventually found and hid. But Seth soon discovered it and tore it into 14 pieces, scattering them in different parts of the country. Isis once again embarked on a journey to find the fragments. Having successfully

Anubis weighing a heart while Thoth records the verdict.
Behind Thoth, a hungry and terrifying Amenti waits eagerly.

gathered them together, she miraculously turned into a kite, and using the wind in her wings, breathed life back into the body of her husband. Isis subsequently gave birth to a son, Horus, who would avenge his father's death by defeating Seth and seizing the Egyptian throne for himself. Isis was worshipped as the most important Egyptian goddess and venerated as the ideal mother. For his part, Osiris remained in the land of the spirits where he became the much revered and powerful god of the afterworld.

It was Osiris who presided over the momentous Trial and Last Judgement, upon which the eternal survival of the soul depended. Summoned before Osiris, seated at his throne, a dead person would undergo the rigors of an intense examination, declaring that he had led a good life and abstained from wrong-doings. The dramatic moment came as the deceased's heart was weighed against the Feather of Truth by the jackal-headed god of the dead, Anubis. If the deceased was found to be free of guilt and to have lived an exemplary life, he would be permitted safe passage to the afterlife. However, those who were deemed to have lived dishonest lives would suffer the fate of being devoured by Amenti, a terrifying god with a crocodile head and a half-lion, half-hippopotamus body.

The Invasion of the Hyksos

After centuries of stability, Egypt once more suffered a reversal of fortune and entered into its Second Intermediate Period. This time, a breakdown in central government had severely weakened the country, leaving it vulnerable to attacks from outside forces. The key challenge came from a group of warlike chariot-driving Semitic nomads who stormed into Egypt from the east via Palestine. Known as the Hyksos ("rulers of foreign lands"), they began to settle in the eastern Delta region to carve out their own kingdom in the land.

In time, the Hyksos adopted Egyptian customs and their leaders even assumed the role of pharaohs, but they were always considered to be foreigners by the Egyptians. They were remembered by ancient Egyptians as invaders who had ruthlessly burned cities and "razed to the ground the temples of the gods and treated all the natives with hostility."

Once again, it was a powerful new Theban dynasty of warrior pharaohs who, after uniting the forces of Upper Egypt, rose up against the invaders and eventually expelled them from the country.

The New Kingdom

The traumatic interlude of the Hyksos fundamentally altered the course of Egyptian history. It had demonstrated the need for a comprehensive military policy to prevent future foreign

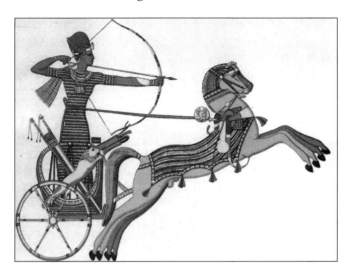

The horse and chariot were introduced into Egypt by the Hyksos.
Pictured here is Pharaoh Ramses II riding into battle.

invasions. Whereas previously there had been no pharaonic policy of expansion beyond the confines of the Nile Valley and Delta, the new warrior kings marched their armies into neighboring territories to secure their borders from future attack, establishing permanent military bases and forcing local powers to recognize their authority and to pay tribute. It marked the beginning of a sustained period of military expansion that brought an end to centuries of political isolation and turned Egypt into a true empire. At its peak, the new Egyptian empire, with its capital at Thebes, extended into territories including Nubia and Syria.

Unwittingly, the Hyksos had played a part in Egypt's ascendancy. Despite having achieved little during their rule, they can be credited for introducing the Egyptians to some

View of the Karnak temple complex.

indispensable innovations—the horse and chariot, the powerful composite bow, and bronze weapons.

At the height of its glory, Thebes was a spectacular city, producing some of the best architecture seen in Egypt since the construction of the pyramids in the Old Kingdom. The vast and wonderful Karnak temple complex, dedicated to the principal Theban god Amun-Ra, was an enormously influential religious center. For more than a thousand years, successive pharaohs made their own contribution to what is now one of the most spectacular of Egypt's monuments. Covering an area of five acres, the temple includes shrines, courtyards, and a succession of huge gateways standing as high as 100 feet.

The New Kingdom also coincided with the rule of Akhenaten, a highly individualistic pharaoh, who caused something of a stir during his lifetime. Originally known as Amenhotep IV, the pharaoh rebelled against the religious traditions of the day. He insisted on the exclusive worship of Aten, a sun god, to the exclusion of all other gods. The priesthood, dedicated to the national god Amun Ra, was incensed. Relations deteriorated to the point where the pharaoh abandoned the city and founded his own capital Aketaten, meaning "the Horizon of Aten."

Amenhotep IV, who now went by the name of Akhenaten, seems not only to have staged a religious revolution, but also an artistic one. The Egyptian artistic convention of presenting pharaohs as perfectly proportioned god-like images was turned on its head. Instead, Akhenaten and his wife Nefertiti were portrayed in a grossly distorted way, with distended stomachs and ill-proportioned limbs. It seems that the pharaoh positively reveled in being portrayed with mortal imperfections.

It was only after Akhenaten IV's young son-in-law succeeded him that things finally returned to normal and the rift between the ruling family and the priesthood was healed. The boy-pharaoh, originally known as *Tut-ankh-aten* meaning "the living image of Aten," was taken under the wing of the influential priesthood, and was given the name *Tut-ankh-amun* in honour of Amun-Ra. The worship of Amun-Ra as the national god was once again restored, and the capital reverted to Thebes.

Born around 1370 B.C., Tutankhamun died while still in his late teens, most likely after suffering a blow to the head in a hunting accident or in battle. Yet, despite his short reign, his enduring fame was secured by the discovery of his wonderful tomb, which lay in a pristine condition for more than 3,000 years. Its discovery in 1922, at the Valley of the Kings in Thebes (at present-day Luxor), caused an international sensation, yielding a wealth of treasures that left the archeologists who first laid eyes on it speechless.

The tomb was not by any means large, nor had work on its construction been completed. But unlike so many others that had been plundered and emptied down the years, Tutankhamun's had mercifully been spared the same fate and its contents left intact. (Although a couple of break-ins did in fact take place shortly after his death, the tomb had been resealed immediately.)

Inside the tomb were thousands of precious artifacts intended to help the pharaoh's spirit in the afterlife. These ranged from pieces of furniture and toys used by the king in his own lifetime, along with vases, amulets, golden statues and jewelry. Tutankhamun's body was placed in three coffins, one inside the other, and then laid to rest in a stone sarcophagus. The innermost coffin, the one that actually contained the king's mummified body, was made of solid gold and weighed 296 pounds.

While Tutankhamun's fame lies not in the circumstances of his short life but in his death, Ramses II, another New Kingdom pharaoh, lived a long and extremely fruitful life that left an indelible print on Egyptian history. Belonging to the 19th dynasty, Ramses II's 67-year reign constituted one of the longest in the country's history, during which time he successfully pursued imperial wars against the Hittite Empire in Asia Minor that had been attacking Syria. Not to be outdone by his predecessors, Ramses II left his own contribution to Egyptian

One the golden chariots found in Tutankhamun's Tomb (now in the Cairo Museum).

Tutankhamun's golden innermost coffin
(now in the Cairo Museum).

architecture by ordering the construction of a massive temple in the far south of the country, at Abu Simbel. The magnificent Temple of Ramses II was carved into a cliff of solid rock and features four colossal seated statues of himself as a young man, each of which stood 65 feet high. Wonderfully detailed relief paintings were added to the walls of the central hallway, including including battle scenes depicting the pharaoh and the Egyptian army in battle scenes against the Nubians and Syrians. A smaller temple was also constructed for Ramses II's favorite wife, Nefertari, and its facade features tall, standing statues of the royal couple.

The Temple of Ramses II at Abu Simbel, showing the colossal seated figures of the pharaoh himself.

The Decline of the Egyptian Pharaohs

Ultimately, Ramses II and his successors were unable to pull Egypt out of what would prove to be a long and steady decline, bringing to an end the glorious age of the Egyptian pharaohs. During the 20th dynasty, towards the end of the 2nd millennium B.C., the Egyptian empire began to falter under the strain of repeated attacks by Mediterranean invaders known only as "Peoples of the Sea," who crossed over from the region of Greece and attacked Egypt from the north or via Libya in the west. The Third Intermediate Period was now upon Egypt.

As one weak dynasty followed another, the country slid into anarchy. Competing dynasties, including one founded by priests and another by a Libyan prince, began to tear the country apart. Eventually, in 667 B.C., the country was invaded by the Assyrians, a neighboring Middle Eastern empire with a reputation for ruthlessness and, for a brief while, they dominated the country. The Egyptians fought back and momentarily reestablished their rule, only to be invaded once more, in 525 B.C., by the powerful Persian Empire, which reduced their country to the status of a mere province. Despite initially respecting the customs and traditions of the ancient Egyptians, the new Persian rulers became heavy-handed once they had consolidated their power. A series of anti-Persian uprisings culminated in a brief spell of renewed Egyptian independence, only to be dashed by yet another Persian invasion in 341 B.C.

Barely a decade later, in 332 B.C., a 25-year-old Greek commander, known to the Western world as Alexander the Great, scored a series of defeats against the Persians and heralded in a new phase of Egyptian history. Alexander was the young ruler of a group of united Greek city states. He had shown himself to be a

Warriors from the ruthless Assyrian Empire that briefly ruled over Egypt.

The oasis town of Siwa, where Alexander the Great consulted the oracle of Amun.

brilliant military commander and was in the process of building himself a huge empire. Jubilant at having been liberated from their Persian overlords, the Egyptians gave Alexander a hero's welcome.

In Egypt, Alexander made the difficult journey to Siwa to consult the famous oracle of Amun. It was a highly significant act for the Greek commander, who had dreamed in his youth that he was the son of Amun. Fortunately, his divine birth was confirmed by the oracle. Satisfied, the priests of Amun accorded him the honor of a deity, and he was accepted as the new pharaoh of Egypt.

Yet the ambitious Alexander had pressing military engagements elsewhere, and the following year he left Egypt to wage campaigns in the Middle East and the Indus Valley, in present-day Pakistan.

The young commander's phenomenal career was cut short by a fever in 323 B.C. before he ever had the chance to return to Egypt. Following his death, his empire was divided amongst his most powerful generals. Egypt went to his close friend and companion, Ptolemy. The Egyptians, unaware of the extent to which they would lose their independence, were quite happy to accept him as Alexander's heir and to proclaim him their new pharaoh.

The arrival of the Greeks dealt the final blow to the pharaonic age. Whereas before, the Egyptians had successfully pulled themselves out of periods of sustained crisis and reestablished their own dynasties, it would be a long time before the country would be ruled by native rulers once more. The Greeks were now in Egypt to stay, and for the next 300 years, it was Ptolemy's successors who would hold sway over the country.

GREEK AND ROMAN EGYPT

The Ptolemies

The first century of Ptolemaic rule proved to be one of stability and prosperity. The new Greek rulers governed the country from the Mediterranean city of Alexandria and their navy dominated the region. From now on Egypt's fortunes would be very much tied to the ancient civilizations of southern Europe. The capital's administration was closely modeled on Athens, giving it a specifically Greek character. Its location ensured that it would blossom into one of the greatest and most influential cultural centers in the classical Greek and, later, Roman world.

Alexandria boasted a library the likes of which had never been seen before. Founded in 330 B.C., it included some 700,000 scrolls, outmatching the very library in Athens that it was designed to emulate. For many centuries it continued to be an institution of great importance, until it was burned down in 640 during the Arab conquest.

The library also included a state-funded teaching institution, famed for its excellence in the field of science and medicine. It was home to a host of brilliant scholars who did much to contribute to our knowledge of the world. Amongst its most famous luminaries were the mathematician Euclid (*c.* 330-260 B.C.), whose theories were to form the basis of mathematical thought for the next 2,000 years; the Greek geographer and mathematician Eratosthenes, (*c.* 276-194 B.C.) who was the first to include lines of longitude and latitude on a map and who calculated the diameter of the earth to within a ten percent margin of error; and the Egyptian astronomer and geographer Claudius Ptolemaeus, known simply as

Ptolemy (*c.* 100-170 A.D.), who developed the widely accepted theory that the earth was at the center of the universe and was orbited by the sun, moon, and stars. Not until the 16th century did the Polish astronomer Copernicus successfully challenge the theory.

A large community of Jews also flourished in Alexandria, many of whom had arrived as mercenaries hired by the Ptolemies. The majority eventually adopted the Greek language, and it was these Alexandrian Jews who were responsible for producing the *Septuagint*, the most important Greek version of the Old Testament, in the 3rd century B.C. On the orders of Ptolemy II, the work was undertaken by Hebrew scholars living on the Island of Pharos in the Bay of Alexandria.

On the same island, Egypt boasted another of the Seven Wonders of the World: a huge lighthouse, also built on the orders of Ptolemy II. It stood 450 feet high, making it the tallest building of its time, and was said to have been visible at a distance of 40 miles. Sadly nothing remains of it today—it was seriously damaged in 793 A.D. and completely destroyed by an earthquake in 1375.

Despite their undeniably successful first years, the Ptolemies were never quite able to emulate the glory of the great Egyptian pharaohs. The most successful of their predecessors had enjoyed the support of a population that identified with them intimately, both on a cultural and religious level, making the task of ruling much easier.

Overall, there was little mixing between the Greeks and Egyptians. The official language of the Ptolemies was Greek, and only Cleopatra, the last of the Ptolemaic rulers, ever learned to speak the native Egyptian tongue. The Greeks were afforded special privileges and formed the core of the state bureaucracy. The Ptolemies were also heavily dependent on the Greeks for their armies. The Egyptians, on the other hand, found themselves excluded from important government posts, and subject to restrictions on where they could settle. With segregation as the rule, intermarriage was not common.

Not that the foreign Ptolemies made no attempt to bridge the gap between themselves and the world of the Egyptians. There was indeed a significant degree of cultural synthesis, especially with regard to religion. Indeed, the kings continued to assume sun-king titles and readily embarked on a program of constructing temples dedicated to Egyptian gods, making sure to keep the priesthood in the manner to which it was accustomed. The almost perfectly preserved Temple of Horus, at Edfu in the Aswan region, is one such example. Built in the 3rd century B.C., its walls feature scenes from ancient Egyptian mythology, including a depiction of Horus's victory over the evil Seth. The Ptolemies also adopted traditional Egyptian funerary practices, including mummification, but added a twist of their own, adorning their coffins with additional Greek features.

Keeping religious traditions alive was not just a matter of piety, however, but also an important way of legitimizing their rule and maintaining social divisions. The Ptolemies' prime concern was to ensure, by means

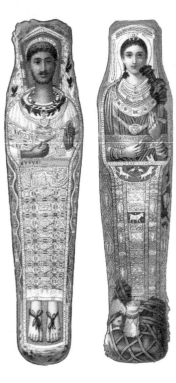

The mummies of a wealthy couple from Ptolemaic times.

The Ptolemaic Temple of Horus, Edfu.

of stiff taxes, a steady flow of wealth into the state coffers, enabling them to maintain their expensive capital, army and fleet.

In time, the Ptolemies found themselves with a disgruntled population on their hands. Soon dissatisfaction gave way to bitter resentment, which in turn erupted into a succession of rebellions that seriously challenged the government's ability to control the country. After losing Upper Egypt the Ptolemies were forced to ease some of their restrictive policies against the Egyptians, allowing them to take up certain posts in government and granting temples a greater degree of freedom. However, keeping the kingdom together had become a near impossible task by this time. Indeed, Ptolemy XII, Cleopatra's father, had come to the conclusion that the dangers for his children were so great, that he found it necessary to put them under the guardianship of the Roman Senate.

Cleopatra—Queen of the Nile

The romantic exploits of Cleopatra VII have long held a great fascination for the Western world and ensured her status as an enduring legend. Most likely born in 68 B.C., she was Ptolemy XII's oldest living daughter. In 51 B.C., according to her father's wishes, she and her younger brother, Ptolemy XIII were married to each other (as was the royal custom in ancient Egypt), and crowned king and queen of Egypt.

Cleopatra, the last in a series of Ptolemaic queens to have borne that name, would prove to be an able leader with a shrewd and ruthless character. On coming to the throne, she ran into serious difficulties as her relationship with her brother and his cronies turned sour. Palace rivalries and disputes soon became so intense that she was forced to flee to Syria in 49 B.C. Undeterred, Cleopatra resolved to enlist the support of a powerful Roman commander she knew had the power to restore her to the throne—Julius Caesar.

At the time, Caesar was staying in Alexandria, where he had come in pursuit of his rival Pompey. On seeing the Egyptian royal family so bitterly divided, Caesar had taken upon himself, as a representative of the Rome, to mediate. With her brother threatening to have her killed, Cleopatra had to use all her guile to get an audience with the Roman commander. Arriving in Alexandria in great secrecy, she had herself rolled up in a carpet and smuggled into his presence. Caesar, now in his fifties, was apparently delighted at the pretty 19-year-old queen's antics and instantly became infatuated with her. Before long, the two had become lovers and the affair resulted in a son, whom they named Caesarion.

Cleopatra now had a formidable ally in Caesar, and together

they defeated her brother's forces, killing him in the process. Having regained the Egyptian throne, she then married her eleven-year-old brother, Ptolemy XIV.

In 46 B.C. Cleopatra and Caesarion joined Caesar in Rome, but the arrangement was short-lived. Caesar's bloody assassination two years later forced both mother and child to return home. In an attempt to strengthen her rule in Egypt, Cleopatra allegedly had her younger brother poisoned and replaced by Caesarion, then only four years old.

Three years later, she was summoned to Tarsus (in modern-day Turkey) to meet Marc Antony. A member of the ruling Triumvirate, he had been given the task of bringing the eastern portion of the Roman

Cleopatra VII, Queen of Egypt.

Empire under control. Cleopatra was determined to keep Rome an ally and endeavored to make her appearance as spectacular as possible. She floated up river to meet Antony, dressed as Aphrodite, the Greek goddess of love, in a magnificent gold-adorned boat with purple sails and silver oars. By all accounts, Antony was thoroughly captivated by the Egyptian queen and did not hesitate to accept an invitation to be her guest in Alexandria.

The two became lovers and Cleopatra spared no expense to ensure that Antony enjoyed his several months in Egypt, organizing banquets that became legendary for their size. Taking a break from all the splendor the royal palace had to offer, it seems the two took to amusing themselves by dressing as commoners and wandering the streets of Alexandria, drinking and playing pranks on unsuspecting victims.

The following year, after Antony had left for Rome, Cleopatra bore him two twins. Although Antony subsequently married another woman, the two were united once more in 36 B.C. and Cleopatra once again became pregnant, giving birth to a boy. In 34 B.C., at a magnificent ceremony in which Cleopatra appeared dressed as the Egyptian goddess Isis, Antony proclaimed her and and Caesarion joint rulers of Egypt and Cyprus. Furthermore, her three young children by Antony were declared rulers over other Roman provinces in the east. These acts flew in the face of caution, provoking the wrath of Anthony's rivals in Rome who claimed he had no business handing over territories to Egypt. Soon war broke out between Antony and Cleopatra's forces and those of Octavian, the future Roman emperor. The couple were soon defeated.

Back in Alexandria, faced with a hopeless situation, Antony and Cleopatra were left to ponder their fate. Antony chose to end his life in the honorable Roman fashion, by falling on his sword. In 30 B.C., towards the end of August, rather than suffer the indignity of being carried off to Rome in chains, Cleopatra took the equally desperate measure of having herself bitten by an asp. Her method of suicide was chillingly calculated. After testing various deadly poisons and venoms on condemned prisoners, she concluded the bite of the asp brought about the quickest and least painful death.

Cleopatra was buried as she had wished, by her lover's side. Her suicide and the subsequent execution of her son Caesarion brought down the final curtain on the Greek Ptolemaic era. The new power in the land from now on was Rome.

Roman Egypt

Egypt was brought under direct Roman domination in 30 B.C., becoming a province of an empire so vast that it had turned the Mediterranean Sea into little more than a Roman lake. For the first two hundred years, Egypt remained relatively stable under the new rulers.

The country was primarily of interest to the Romans for its agricultural produce, and came to supply enough grain to satisfy a third of Rome's needs. The grain was collected as a tax paid in kind. With efficient agricultural production already up and running, they saw little point in interfering too much with the existing Ptolemaic administration, and even kept Greek as the official language. The Romans simply placed themselves in the highest positions of power and left the rest of the hierarchy intact, with the Greeks and Jews next in the social ladder and the Egyptians at the bottom. Like the Ptolemies before them, they taxed the native population excessively hard and, in some cases, the burden was so great that there were reports of whole villages disappearing as they fled the clutches of the tax collectors.

The country's major port through which nearly all trade with Rome passed was Alexandria. In addition to grain, Egypt was also an important exporter of papyrus and red granite, which was quarried in Aswan. It was also in Alexandria that the Romans faced their first serious challenge. The port had gained itself a reputation as a hotbed of political activism as various factions within its complex multi-ethnic society struggled to win concessions and power. The Greeks on their part bitterly resented the erosion of special privileges they had inherited from the Ptolemaic times and were outraged by Roman favoritism towards the Jews. In the early part of the 2nd century A.D., tensions between the Greek and Jewish communities culminated in massacres of Jews. Soon afterwards, the Egyptians, who bitterly resented working like slaves to feed mouths in Rome, also staged a series of revolts and further tested Rome's ability to maintain control over its province.

Had the ruling elite capitalized on the traditional relationship between the pharaoh and the population, they might have found the task of governing somewhat easier. Their predecessors, the Ptolemies, had been careful to continue the tradition of identifying themselves with the sun-god, thereby helping to strengthen the ties between the people and the state. Yet, the Roman emperors did no such thing. They remained aloof and few even bothered to set foot in the country.

In such a changing political climate, the temple communities, which had been the guardians of the old social traditions, found themselves with an ever-dwindling number of believers. As they hit hard times, their temples gradually fell into disuse. Meanwhile, a new religion was making its presence felt in the land, one that would deliver an even bigger blow to the ancient religious beliefs and ways of life—Christianity.

The Copts and Early Christianity

Christianity is traditionally believed to have been introduced into Egypt by the evangelist St. Mark in the first century A.D. By this time, Roman Egypt had already been the setting of one of the great Biblical events—the flight of Mary, Joseph and the infant Jesus from Palestine to Egypt in order to escape the reign of terror under Herod.

Monastery of St. Catherine at the foot of
Mount Sinai.

However, not until the 2nd and 3rd centuries would the new religion firmly take root in Egypt, eventually finding a fertile ground that would greatly nourish its spiritual and intellectual development.

The Christians of Egypt became known as Copts, a word that is derived from the Arabic *Qibt*, itself a corruption of the Greek *Aigyptos* meaning "Egypt." When the Arabs conquered the land in the 7th century, they referred to it as *Dar al-Qibt* meaning "Home of the Copt." By this time, Christianity had become so widespread that the Arabs made no distinction between Christian or Egyptian, and used the word "Copt" interchangeably.

These early Christians brought their own special character to the religion, and in the early years suffused it with the old pagan culture of the land. In fact, even the form of the cross they adopted as a symbol of their faith was a modified version of an ankh, the hieroglyph used during the pharaonic times as the sign of "eternal life."

As happened in other parts of the Roman Empire, members of this new subversive religion faced terrifying treatment at the hands of a regime that was set on eradicating it. The first wave of persecution began under the Roman emperor Decius in the middle of the 3rd century. Tough new laws were passed which made failure to attend pagan temples a serious offence. Not complying could

A Coptic tile dating from the 6th century.

result in torture and even death. As the persecution intensified, more and more Christians fled to the safety of the desert, where eventually flourishing monastic communities would appear. The situation deteriorated in 303 A.D., when, after a period of respite, the Roman emperor Diocletian ordered the burning of bibles and the destruction of all churches. Soon edicts were passed that unleashed a new round of imprisonment, torture and the deaths of thousands of Egyptians. In commemoration of this profoundly traumatic period of their history, the Copts dated their calendar from 284 A.D.—the year of Diocletian's succession—and named their era the "Age of the Martyrs."

One of the Church's most famous martyrs was the legendary St. Catherine of Alexandria, who was executed in the 4th century. An educated woman from a family of high standing, she fell afoul of the authorities for criticizing the worship of idols. After steadfastly refusing to recant, she was tied to a wheel, tortured and decapitated. According to popular belief, her remains were found some 400 years later at Mount Sinai, and buried by monks in the Monastery of St. Catherine at the foot of the holy mountain (reputed to be the same mountain where Moses received the Ten Commands from God). St. Catherine became the patron saint of young men, lawyers, scholars and wheelwrights.

Early on, Alexandria emerged as the bustling hub of Christian learning. Its Catechetical School, founded around 190 A.D., boasted a center for studies including the sciences, mathematics and humanities. Its first head, Pantaenus, was a leading figure in the development of the use of the Greek alphabet to transcribe the native language, Coptic. The new alphabet greatly facilitated the study and rendering of the Gospels. Until then, the language had been written using the Egyptian demotic script, which although a substantially simplified form of hieroglyphic and hieratic script, was nevertheless too unwieldy for everyday use. Since there were certain sounds in the native language that had no corresponding Greek letter, seven additional demotic signs had to be retained to make up the short-fall.

In time, students and clergy from around the world flocked to the city to receive instruction from some of the greatest Christian scholars of the time, one of whom was Origen, regarded by many as the father of theology. Born in Alexandria around 185 A.D., Origen's family was tragically affected by the Roman persecution of Christians. At the age of 17, his own father was arrested and beheaded by the authorities. This did nothing to dampen Origen's own belief, however, and he subsequently went on to become a prolific writer in the field of Christian theology. His greatest work, entitled the *Hexapla*, brought together, for the first time in history, several Hebrew and Greek texts of the Bible. His works had a profound effect on the early Christian church and today he remains the subject of much study. Origen too suffered at the hands of the Romans for his faith, and was subjected to the horrors of imprisonment and torture. He was later freed but never recovered from his ordeal, and died an exhausted and broken man in about 254 A.D.

For many Christians living under the Romans the tide began to turn during the 4th century, after the Emperor Constantine converted to Christianity and declared it the official religion of the empire. However, in a cruel twist of fate, the Copts were never, in fact, to enjoy the new-found religious freedom, but were destined to experience yet more persecution at the hands of the Roman authorities.

Upheavals in the Roman Empire at the end of the 4th century had resulted in the creation of two separate empires—west and east, with Rome and Constantinople as their respective capitals. The latter became known as the Byzantine Empire and it was to this realm that Egypt belonged. The Copts found themselves seriously at odds with the Christian Byzantine Empire over their interpretation of the nature of Christ. Whereas the Byzantines held that Christ was both human and divine, the Copts instead believed in his total divinity. Such a view was regarded by the Byzantine authorities as heretical, and the Copts were excommunicated from the Orthodox Church at the Council of Chalcedon in 451. This belief, known as Monophysism, still places the Copts apart from mainstream Christianity today.

The rift in the church lead to a concerted effort by the Byzantine authorities to impose religious uniformity in Egypt with force. From 451 until the Arab conquests, Copts were subjected to prohibitive taxes and ferocious treatment, including torture, supervised by the all-powerful Byzantine governor in Egypt. Undeterred, the Copts gradually came to develop as a unique church, led by their own pope and patriarch in Alexandria.

St. Anthony and Monasticism

Egypt played a vital role in the development of Christian monasticism and the most famous of its Desert Fathers was St. Anthony—a Copt of Egyptian descent, considered by many to be the founder of the institution and "father of all monks." Although not the first to renounce material comforts in favor of a solitary existence spent in spiritual contemplation, his dedication earned him a special place in the Christian world.

Born to a Christian family around 251, Anthony was said to have lived 70 of his 105 years in the solitude of the desert. After the death of his parents, when he was in his late teens, he inherited a considerable amount of land and the responsibility of caring for his young sister. However, after contemplating the Gospel of Matthew and its message urging the renunciation of material wealth, Anthony underwent a profound change and subsequently gave away his possessions. Entrusting his sister to a convent, he left for the solitude of the Eastern Desert of Egypt and embarked on a life-long spiritual quest.

According to St. Athanasius, who knew the saint and wrote his biography, Antony's fame rested "not for his writings, nor for his worldly wisdom, or for any art." Indeed, Anthony never attended school and was illiterate. Instead his reputation relied quite simply on "his reverence for God." His life became the embodiment of his principles of solitude, chastity, and poverty, inspiring numerous followers to leave their homes for the desert in order to follow his example. In time, small informal communities turned into permanent settlements, becoming the first monasteries in Christian history. One of Anthony's contemporaries, St. Pachom, took the step of formally laying down the rules of monastic life. From these humble desert beginnings, monasticism eventually spread to Europe and the rest of the world, where it still remains a way of life for countless monks and nuns.

Interestingly, there is little doubt that Coptic missionaries reached Britain well before St. Augustine of Canterbury embarked on his mission to bring Christianity to the Britons in 597. Egyptian monks were also among the earliest Christians ever to set foot in Ireland.

ISLAMIC EGYPT

In the winter of 639, an Arab army stormed into Egypt from Syria. Its leader was Amr ibn al-As, an extremely capable Muslim general who had played a key role in the massive Arab assault on the Persian and Byzantine empires. Dissatisfied with the spoils of war in Syria, Amr had turned his eager eye towards the spectacular and plunder-rich city of Alexandria. In July 640, after being reinforced by troops from various Arab tribes, he had little difficulty in defeating the Byzantine army at Heliopolis. Nine months later, after a lengthy siege, his army conquered the fortress of Babylon, situated at present-day Cairo. Finally, in September 642, the prized city of Alexandria surrendered. The event ushered in a new age, bringing in its wake a new and powerful religion, Islam.

Egypt under the Umayyad and Abbasid Empires

The Umayyads (r. 661-750), based in the Syrian capital of Damascus, were the first great Muslim Arab dynasty to rule over Egypt. Their leader, known as a caliph, held the highest position of authority in the Muslim temporal world. It was the Umayyads who were responsible for the early spread of Islam, the religion of the 7th-century Prophet Muhammad. The empire they built up was huge, stretching, at its peak, from the borders of China all the way across North Africa to the shores of the Atlantic Ocean. Even Spain was Umayyad territory, and had it not been for the defeat of the Arab army at Poiters in 732, less that 200 miles from Paris, France may well have been incorporated into the Arabic Islamic world too.

For the Copts, the Muslim invasion was a blessing in disguise. The Arabs did not expect the population to convert to Islam, nor were they hostile to Christianity. Indeed, both Christians and Jews were considered to be fellow "Peoples of the Book" (The Old Testament) under Islamic law, and it was the policy of the Arabs to permit them to practice their religion without hindrance or fear of persecution. There was a price to pay, however, and all able-bodied non-Muslim males were required to pay a special tax. They were also forbidden from bearing arms—a measure that was not entirely without benefit, since it exempted them from military service.

The Copts also enjoyed preferential treatment from their new overlords. Under the Byzantines, they had been hounded for their unorthodox views and had come to detest their fellow Christian rulers. It was a division the Arabs readily exploited and, shunning the Byzantine establishment, they lured the pope out from hiding and afforded the Copts special privileges, charging them with the collection of taxes levied on the non-Muslim population.

After a meteoric rise, the Umayyad dynasty came to an abrupt end in 750, when a rival faction, called the Abbasids, staged a revolt and overthrew the Umayyad caliph and his family in Damascus. The caliph attempted to flee but was hunted down and killed in the Egyptian town of Busiris. Eighty other leading Umayyads were butchered after being tricked into attending a banquet.

Ruling from their capital at Baghdad, the new Abbasid dynasty struggled hard to maintain a hold over its empire. By the 9th century, however, the task proved too much as provincial governors began to assert their own power.

In Egypt, the Arab governor Ahmad ibn Tulun acquired a formidable range of political and military powers and, despite professing to recognize the suzerainty of the Abbasids in Baghdad, he effectively ruled as an independent leader beginning in 868. He built up a huge army of as many as a 100,000 men, a large number of which were slaves, and even managed to extend his influence into a good part of Syria.

Rather than channel wealth out of Egypt and into the imperial coffers of Baghdad, Ibn Tulun held on to the taxes he raised and plowed much of the proceeds into a booming program of public works. It was a period that saw the creation of some of the finest architecture in Egypt. The baked brick Mosque of Ibn Tulun, which still stands in Cairo, is famous throughout the Islamic world and features the oldest minaret in the country.

Ibn Tulun wielded such power that he was even able to establish his own dynasty in Egypt, though it was short-lived affair. Once the strong hand of the founder was no longer on the tiller, his successors soon lost their grip on the country. The end came in 905, when the Abbasids stepped in once more and imposed a new governor who was answerable to the caliph. For another few decades Egypt struggled on, subjected to yet another short-lived and semi-independent dynasty, the Ikhshidids. An end to years of uncertainty finally came with the arrival of a powerful new force of religiously fanatical Muslims from the west, the Fatimids.

The Fatimids—Shi'ism versus Sunnism

When the Fatimids finally conquered Egypt in 969, they encountered practically no resistance. They immediately made Cairo, from the Arabic *al -Qahira* meaning "the Victorious One," their new capital. Although they were originally from Tunisia, once they had established their hold over the Egyptians and adopted it as their own power base, the Fatimids brought Egypt a degree of independence it had not enjoyed since the days of the great pharaohs. From Cairo, they pursued a policy of expansion into territories beyond the Egyptian frontiers, boasting governors in eastern Libya, western Saudi Arabia and as far north as

The Minaret of the Mosque of Ibn Tulun in Cairo,
constructed in the 9th century.

The Courtyard of the Mosque of Ibn Tulun.

Damascus in Syria. Furthermore, they commanded the allegiance of local rulers from several other Mediterranean lands.

The Fatimids had not only challenged the political might of the Abbasid caliphate, but also rejected its spiritual authority in the Arab world. The reasons for this are complex, arising from a major disagreement in Islam that led to the creation of two rival Muslim rites, both of which continue to come to loggerheads today. These are known as Sunnism, the orthodox version to which the previous Muslim rulers of Egypt had adhered, and Shi'ism, that professed by the Fatimids.

The main problem centered on a dispute surrounding the leadership of the Muslims after the death of Muhammad, who was held in Islam to be the last and final in a line of prophets that also included Ibrahim (Abraham) and Isa (Jesus).

Muhammad was born in Mecca, on the Arabian peninsula, around 570. A merchant, he began preaching in 616 after experiencing a series of revelations by which God communicated his will through the angel Jibril (Gabriel). These revelations were collected together after his death to make up the sacred book of Islam, the Quran.

Muhammad's followers believed, as they do today, that there is only one god, Allah, and that the faithful should surrender entirely to his will and practice the Five Pillars of Faith: publicly declaring their faith, praying five times a day, giving alms, fasting during the holy month of Ramadam, and making the pilgrimage to Mecca.

However, when Muhammad died in 632, he left no declared successor. In an attempt to fill the void, one of his closest followers, Abu Bakr, was elected caliph, meaning "successor" or "deputy" of Muhammad, the Messenger of God. Three other close followers of Muhammad were subsequently elected to the same position. The last of these was Ali, who had married the prophet's daughter Fatima.

Some argued that Ali alone was the legitimate heir and only those of his line could continue the leadership of the Muslims. After running into strong opposition, Ali was assassinated and his sons were prevented from assuming the role of caliph. Those who believed that the descendants of Ali and Fatima were the rightful successors of Muhammad subsequently became known as Shi'i—from *Shi'at Ali,* meaning Ali's Party. The Sunnis, on the other hand, were those who supported the original line of caliphs and their successors.

During the early period, the Fatimid caliphs and their followers, who believed their masters to be divinely guided figures with a destiny to impose Islamic justice in the world, made a great deal of trouble for the rival Abbasid caliphate in Baghdad. They bullied and cajoled them, sending missionaries to preach to the Abbasid population. In 1058, the Abbasids were even forced to suffer the indignity of acknowledging Fatimid supremacy.

Yet despite their zealousness overseas, the atmosphere in Egypt was, for the most part, considerably more relaxed—especially after they had consolidated their leadership. Life for the majority of the population continued much as it had before. Indeed, Shi'ism as a doctrine was primarily restricted to the elite and never adopted by the population at large.

Islamic Art and Architecture in Egypt

During the early period of Fatimid rule, Egypt flourished economically and culturally, and it was a time during which the country saw some outstanding achievements in the areas of architecture and art. Prior to the Fatimids, Egypt had already seen the construction of the splendid Mosque of Ibn Tulun. It had a fine early example of a minaret, an architectural feature which first appeared in the 7th century. Muhammad had declared that the call

Detail of carved wooden panel from 11th-century Egypt.

to prayer five times a day should be from the highest rooftop nearest to the mosque and, in time, minarets became an integral part of the actual mosque itself.

Another prominent feature of a mosque was the dome, symbolizing the vault of heaven. It was the Fatimids who introduced this innovation into Egypt. The Fatimids incorporated two small domes into their al-Azhar Mosque in Cairo, which they began to build just one year after coming to power. It would prove to be one of their greatest accomplishments and is the oldest surviving building from the Fatimid era. The mosque was soon to become a major center of learning in the Islamic world. Indeed, the institution is still in existence today and lays claim to being the oldest university in the world. Retaining its position as a hugely influential school of

Quranic teaching, the al-Azhar continues to attract Muslim scholars from around the world.

Islamic artists frowned upon representations of living creatures, and instead concentrated their efforts on calligraphy, creating elaborate copies of the Quran. They also developed a style of art known as "arabesque," featuring intricate abstract geometrical and floral designs that were used to great effect on the surfaces of mosques. The Fatimids themselves produced beautiful examples of woodcarvings, bronzes, textiles, and ceramics, adorning them with the likes of stars and plants. Flouting orthodox conventions, the Fatimids did, in fact, include animals in their work, and in some highly imaginative works depicted them being attacked by monsters.

From Glory to Ruin

The pinnacle of Fatimid rule coincided with the enlightened rule of Abu-Mansur Nizar al-Aziz, from 975 to 996. It was a period that saw a boom in the construction of palaces, mosques, bridges and canals in and around Cairo. Under Nizar al-Aziz's rule, the Christians and Jews also enjoyed a great deal of tolerance.

His successor al-Hakim (r. 996-1021) was not so generous, however, and displayed behavior that bordered on madness. Al-Hakim, who became caliph at the young age of 11, launched a campaign of persecution against the Christians and Jews. He confiscated their property and forced them to wear distinctive clothing. Other sections of the population were similarly targeted with a whole array of prohibitions that forbade, among other things, keeping dogs or playing chess. Shoemakers were forbidden to make women's shoes, and any woman unfortunate enough to be caught going to the public baths was liable to find herself bricked up alive in the building itself.

Inside and outside the al-Azhar Mosque, founded by the Fatimids
in the 10th century.

As al-Hakim became ever more extreme and brutal in his policies, he became increasingly unpopular. Finally, his position became untenable. One night, whilst out on a donkey ride, he simply disappeared, never to be seen again—most probably murdered by his own family.

As the years went by, the Fatimid regime began to slide inexorably into an abyss of sustained crises and factional fighting. Abroad, the Fatimids began to lose control over their territories, and at home, real power was being usurped by powerful viziers who ruled in place of inexperienced and ineffectual young caliphs.

Before long, the country was plunged into one of its darkest periods. Caliphs, viziers, and military cliques all vied for the throne, as if engaged in a bizarre and macabre form of musical chairs. Court intrigues, plots and murder became the order of the day, as the country struggled under ever-increasing taxation. The end arrived mercifully in 1171, in the form of one of the greatest leaders in history—Saladin.

Saladin—Hero of the Islamic World

Ayyub Salah al-Din, better known to the Western world as Saladin, was the founder of the Ayyubid dynasty that ruled over Egypt between 1171 and 1250. A brilliant military commander who possessed a deep sense of honor that did not fail to impress even his enemies, Saladin's firm yet just leadership helped unite the Muslims against Christian Europe, winning back for them the holy city of Jerusalem, which had lain under occupation by the Crusader forces for nearly 90 years.

Saladin was born to a Kurdish family in 1138, in Takrit, which lies on the Tigris River in northern present-day Iraq. Though little is known of Saladin's early life, it appears that he was quite taken by the study of the Quran and poetry. At the age of 18 he was made deputy military governor of Damascus, a job that involved maintaining law and order.

Eventually, Saladin began to accompany his uncle, Shirkuh, on military campaigns. Shirkuh was a general in the army of Nur al-Din, an extremely powerful commander who had managed to score a series of successes against the Crusaders and had taken control of Syria. In 1168, Saladin and his uncle waged a successful campaign to fend off a Crusader invasion of Egypt, gaining a great deal of popularity from the population in the process.

As a result of his efforts on behalf of Nur al-Din, Shirkuh was appointed vizier of Egypt, but died shortly afterwards. In 1169, 31-year-old Saladin took the title of vizier for himself and assumed control of the Syrian army in Egypt. He was now much closer to realizing his two burning ambitions: firstly to substitute Shi'ism with the Sunnism in which he had been raised, and secondly to expel the Crusader forces that had for so long occupied extensive territories in the Middle East.

When the Fatimid caliph in Egypt died in 1171, Saladin saw his moment to bring about the first of his dreams. He quietly had the traditional mention of the caliph's name dropped from prayers on Friday, the Muslim holy day of the week, and replaced by that of the Abbasid caliph. With this seemingly simple act, he had begun the process of restoring Sunnism to Egypt.

With the death of Nur al-Din in 1174, Saladin seized his opportunity take control over Syria and turn his attention to the question of the Christian Crusaders.

Saladin, one of the most enduring heroes in the Muslim world.

Background to the First Crusade

The first of the wave of Crusades had taken place some 80 years previously. It originally began as a response to an appeal for help by the Byzantine Emperor in Constantinople to prevent Turkish tribes from further encroaching onto the Eastern frontiers of the Byzantine empire. Pope Urban II, anxious to display the power of the papacy, heeded his call. On November 26, 1095, in a speech made in southern France, he urged Christians to defend the eastern Church and "enter upon the road to the Holy Sepulcher and wrest it from the wicked race and subject it." (The Holy Sepulcher was a cave in Jerusalem where the body of Christ was believed to have lain before resurrection and was marked by a church.)

The response was phenomenal. Within a year, an army of 150,000 had gathered in Constantinople, ready to march against the Muslims. The "army" was in fact a hodgepodge of Europeans from all walks of life, from the lowliest peasant to members of the nobility. Amongst their ranks were romantics, adventurers, and criminals, lured by dreams of making their fortunes overseas, or for some, of dying a martyr's death.

By the summer of 1099, the Crusaders—who had already gained extensive territories along the Eastern Mediterranean coast—were amassing an army of some 20,000 outside the gates of Jerusalem. The Egyptian Fatimid force protecting the city numbered no more than a thousand, and stood little chance. After a month's siege, the Crusaders came storming through the city walls and embarked on an orgy of violence. They butchered thousands of people, Muslims, Jews, and native Christians alike. The defeat, and the dreadful manner in which it was carried out, left a long-lasting feeling of bitterness amongst the Muslims.

Having seized the prize of Jerusalem, the Crusaders set about strengthening their position in the Middle East, carving their new territories into four separate states, including the Kingdom of Jerusalem, which stretched all the way south to the Red Sea.

Saladin and the Capture of Jerusalem

In Saladin, the Crusaders were to find one of their greatest enemies. His commitment to Islam and his firm sense of purpose served as an inspiration to unite the Muslim world, which until now had been fragmented and reeling from the onslaught of the Christian armies. Speaking to his biographer of his dreams for the future, Saladin declared:

> "When by God's help not a Frank is left on this coast, I mean to divide my territories, and to charge [my successors] with my last commands. Then having taken leave of them, I will sail on this sea to its islands in pursuit of them until there shall not remain on this earth one unbeliever in God—or I will die in the attempt!"

Reflecting his spiritual beliefs, Saladin rejected the trappings of fame, living a simple and austere life. Yet, he possessed more than simple religious zeal. He had also gained considerable skills as a commander, and he was soon to put them to good use.

After a series of successful campaigns, in July 1187, Saladin launched his most ambitious offensive against the Crusaders and crushed a huge Crusader army at the Battle of Hattin. Left reeling from the devastating loss in its ranks, the Crusaders were in no shape to withstand Saladin's campaign of sustained attacks on their strongholds. On October 2, after a siege of only one week, the city of Jerusalem surrendered. Mercifully, Saladin chose not to repeat the

The Citadel of Cairo, Saladin's fortified palace complex.

violent abuses carried out by the Crusaders years earlier, and Christians were allowed to leave peacefully. Further victories followed in the wake of this devastating blow, and the Crusader towns fell, one by one, until all but a handful remained. The loss of Jerusalem sent shock waves throughout Europe, and the population of the West clamored to join the third and largest of the Crusades. It was here that Saladin was to pit his wits against another legendary warrior of the time, Richard I, "The Lionheart" of England.

The Crusaders concentrated their efforts on the coastal city of Acre (today in Israel), laying siege to it by land and sea. In July 1191, after two long years, the city finally surrendered to the Crusaders. Saladin's previous demonstration of mercy was not reciprocated, however, and Richard the Lionheart had several thousand of his captives killed after failing to receive an agreed-upon ransom.

Not for the want of trying, the English king never in fact succeeded in capturing Jerusalem. Instead he was forced to make a truce with Saladin. In the resulting peace talks, it was agreed that the Crusaders would keep control of the coastal territories, while the Muslims would retain the interior lands and permit Christians safe access to pilgrim sites.

Months after peace was restored in the Middle East, Saladin was struck down by fever. He died on March 4, 1193, at the age of 55. It was said that in his final moments he had a smile on his face that anticipated paradise. He was buried in Damascus.

The Ayyubids—Saladin's Sunni Heirs

Though its founder was gone, the Ayyubid dynasty continued to exercise firm control over Egypt, at least for the first few years. After the dark final days of the Fatimids, Saladin and his descendants breathed a new lease of life into Egypt, and ushered in a period of economic and cultural revival.

A significant development, initiated by Saladin himself, was the replacement of Shi'i institutions with those of the Sunni rite, thus eradicating Fatimid influence and promoting orthodox Sunnism, which remains the dominant form of Islam in Egypt to this day. To this end, the Ayyubids founded numerous *madrasas*—which became the cornerstone of religious life in Egypt. *Madrasas* were teaching mosques, or religious colleges, dedicated to training religious lawyers whose task it was to interpret Islamic *sharia* law. Every aspect of Muslim life was regulated according to the *sharia*, including marriage, inheritance, property and the conduct of business. *Sharia* law, however, did not embrace the whole population. Only Muslims came under its jurisdiction, while Christians and Jews continued to apply their own local laws according to their own customs and traditions.

Although Arabic had been the official language in Egypt since 706, Coptic, the late variant of the ancient Egyptian language, continued to be spoken as an everyday language up until the 13th century. Indeed, scribes even continued the practice of writing certain documents in both Coptic and Arabic. By the beginning of the 14th century, however, the language had declined to the point that it was used almost exclusively for religious purposes. To this day, it remains the language of Copt church services.

Under *Sharia* law, Christians and Jews continued to live as protected minorities under the Muslims. Yet, as minorities they were always subject to additional taxation and certain restrictions. Saladin himself reintroduced special rules, requiring them to wear clothes that distinguished them from the Muslim population—in the case of the Christians, this meant wearing black turbans and large crosses. Furthermore, although educated Copts might find opportunities to better their social standing by securing positions in government, the majority of Christians belonged to the poorest sections of the population.

Title page of a 14th-century manuscript written in both Arabic
(right) and Coptic (left)—a language descended from
Ancient Egyptian, written using the Greek alphabet,
with the addition of seven demotic letters.

Despite a period of backsliding, the Ayyubids went on to score a series of successes against the Crusaders. This was especially so in the case of the Sixth Crusade, which suffered a crushing defeat at the hands of the Egyptians. The ill-fated Crusader army had optimistically marched into Egypt only to be defeated at Cairo in April 1250. They suffered the further humiliation of seeing their leader, King Louis IX of France, taken hostage along with many of his nobles, and held for ransom for a million gold dinars. Only after the enormous sum was paid was the unfortunate king released.

However, the Ayyubids were destined to come to an ignominious end. Immersed in a quagmire of intrigue and murder, it was they who had unwittingly set the scene for their own doom. Their practise of importing and training Turkish slaves, called Mamluks, to serve as the Sultan's personal elite corp had created a powerful military force that was soon to turn against them.

The end came as Egypt found itself governed by an ex-slave girl of Armenian descent by the name of Shajar al-Durr (meaning "Sea of Pearls"). Shajar al-Durr was the widow of the sultan al-Salih Ayyub, and had connived with the Mamluks to have her stepson ruler murdered and herself placed on the throne in 1250. Yet, she found herself in a precarious position. Not since Cleopatra had a woman ruled Egypt, and the idea of a female leader was the source of considerable unease amongst the ruling elite. Shajar al-Durr's original owner was no less than the Abbasid caliph in Baghdad, who roared that if no man in Egypt was up to the task of being the sultan than he would personally come to Cairo and bring them one. The problem was subsequently solved by the marriage of Shajar al-Durr to the chief Mamluk, al-Din Aybak, an act that put state power directly into the hands of the Mamluks.

Shajar al-Durr and Sultan Aybak's rule lasted nearly a decade, but degenerated into a murderous frenzy in 1259. After discovering that Aybak planned to take a second wife, Shajar al-Durr had him brutally murdered. Three days later she too lay dead—battered to death with wooden bath shoes. Her body was then thrown from a tower by the slave women of Aybak's ex-wife, whom he had divorced in favor of Shajar al-Durr. Her death brought to an end the Ayyubid chapter of Egyptian history. The power vacuum it created was readily filled by another powerful Mamluk warlord, and for many years to come this unusual warrior class would establish their own dynasties and rule directly over Egypt.

The Mamluks—A Dynasty of Former Slaves

For 250 years the Mamluks were the indisputable masters of Egypt, ruling over one of the most war-torn and troubled regions of those times. Never that many in numbers, their success rested on their formidable military skills.

The Mamluks (from the Arabic meaning "owned" or "possessed") were slaves of foreign birth who had traditionally been used by the Ayyubids as an elite military force. They were highly trained cavalrymen, whose skills in archery made them a formidable opponent in the battlefield. Once in power, the Mamluks themselves continued to import slaves, replenishing their ranks with raw recruits. Such an unusual practice worked in the Mamluks' favor. Uprooted from their homes at a young age and with no attachment to the unfamiliar land, they soon developed a fierce loyalty to their masters and comrades in arms.

The novice Mamluks were converted to Islam and put through a grueling and often dangerous training regime that lasted up to ten years. They learned the art of controlling a horse using their knees, thus leaving their hands free to fire arrows at targets, which they could do seated, and facing the front or the back. In order to build up their arm muscles they would be required to slice lumps of clay up to a thousand times a day with their swords. Polo was also an activity employed to develop their considerable riding skills. Once they had successfully completed their training, the young slaves were given their freedom and could look forward to a comfortable future in the ranks of the ruling elite—some becoming extremely wealthy in the process.

Mamluk rule in Egypt is traditionally divided into two stages: the Bahri Period, which lasted from 1250 to 1382, and the Burgi Period, from 1382 until 1517. The Bahri Mamluks took their name from the

The medieval streets of Cairo, much as they would have appeared in the Mamluk era.

Arabic *bahr*, meaning "sea" or "river," on account of the fact that their barracks lay on an island in the Nile. It was this group, made up of Qipchaq Turks from the northern shores of the Black Sea in present-day southern Russia, who provided the country with sultans during the first period of Mamluk rule.

During the second period, the sultans were chosen from the Burgi Mamluks, warrior Circassians who came from the region of the northwest Caucasus, west of the Black Sea. They derived their name from the Arabic *burj*, meaning "tower," since their barracks lay in the towered Citadel of Cairo.

Rivalry between these two factions of Mamluks was intense and often led to bitter and murderous feuds. Indeed, during two-and-a-half centuries of their rule, 20 out of a total of 54 Mamluk sultans came to a violent end, either murdered or executed. Of the rest only ten saw through their natural days in office; the remainder were deposed. Nevertheless, during the early part their rule at least, under the stronger government of the Bahri sultans, Egypt enjoyed periods of prosperity.

It was the Bahri Mamluks that were responsible for checking the onslaught of the ferocious and terrifying Mongols in 1258, after the latter had stormed into Persia from the steppes of Central Asia and captured the supposedly impregnable capital of Baghdad. Thousands upon thousands of Muslims were butchered mercilessly in the streets of the city—only the Jews and Christians were spared. After forcing the caliph to reveal where he had hidden his treasure, the Mongols had him rolled up in a carpet and trampled to death under the hooves of their horses. The once great capital was left in ruins—its palaces, mosques and other institutions utterly destroyed. After the carnage in Baghdad, the Mongols rode on to Damascus, with their sights set on Egypt.

However, the Mongols had not counted on the ruthless Baybars, a giant Mamluk who sported a cataract in one of his blue eyes. It was Baybars, destined to become the first great Mamluk sultan, who would be remembered in history as the man who put an end Mongol expansion in the Middle East. In 1260, he marched his army into Palestine and defeated their army at the Battle of Ayn Jalut. For centuries after his death, the Mamluk warlord remained a popular folk hero whose exploits were mythologized in colorfully exaggerated tales of bravery.

After murdering the sultan, Baybars took the title for himself, and set about strengthening his power in Egypt. He also launched successful military campaigns against the Crusaders and splinter

Arab territories in Syria, in addition to preventing further incursions by the Mongols. Showing a flair for diplomacy, Baybars managed to legitimize his rule by rescuing the uncle of the murdered Abbasid caliph and declaring him caliph in Cairo. But from this point forward, the caliphs, shorn of the powers they once possessed, would be answerable to the Mamluks alone. Baghdad's prestigious role as the center of the Arab world had suffered a great blow, and Mamluk Egypt now became the major power that linked the East with the West.

Baybars died in 1277, it appears after drinking too much of his favorite alcoholic beverage, fermented mare's milk—although there was talk of poison. His son succeeded him to the office of sultan, but his reign would be short-lived. Within three years, a Mamluk military commander by the name of Qalawun seized power.

Qalawun established a dynasty that was to last for a century. Like Baybars, Qalawun earned himself a reputation for his military successes against the Mongols and Christian Crusader states, the latter of which he reduced to a small territory surrounding Acre. The job was finished by his son and successor Khalil, who, in 1293, had the last of the beleaguered Crusaders scurrying off in full retreat to Cyprus.

Although another of Qalawun's sons, Al-Nasir Muhammad, managed a fairly lengthy, if not continuous, reign between 1294 and 1340, from this time on the ruling elite became decidedly unruly. The following series of sultans were unable to disentangle themselves from the extremely fractious politics of the time. Around them powerful and murderous emirs fought each other for power, turning the sultans themselves into little more than puppets.

In 1382, as the leadership degenerated further into bitter feuding, Barquq, a Circassian emir from the barracks in the Citadel managed to seized the throne for himself. The new sultan

Interior views of the Sultan Hassan Mosque. Built between 1356 and 1360, it is one of the largest mosques in the world.

then handed out positions of authority to those who shared his origins, marking the beginning of the Burgi period of Mamluk rule, which would last until 1517.

The Mamluks, especially under the Bahris, injected a vigor of their own into the cultural life of Egypt, founding a wonderful legacy of architecture in Cairo that included mosques, mausoleums, forts, and caravanserais (the name given to an inn built around a large court that accommodated caravans in the Middle and Far East). Both Qalawun and his successor Muhammad al-Nasir proved to be important patrons of architecture. So too did Sultan Hassan, who reigned between 1347 and 1361, and whose mosque is considered to be one of the finest built by the Mamluks and the most important monument in Cairo.

Street life outside the Mosque of Sultan Hassan.

Egypt also continued to be a vital center for learning, and under the patronage of Barquq and his successors the country became the adopted home of a man generally considered to be the most influential thinker in classical Islam—Ibn Khaldun.

Ibn Khaldun

Born in Tunis (in Tunisia) on May 27, 1332, Abu Zaid Abdel Rahman ibn Khaldun led a colorful and exciting life in the stormy world of Arabic politics, the dangers of which eventually led to his arrival in Egypt. His wayfaring life offers a wonderful example of the interconnectedness of the Arabic world to which Egypt belonged, where the Arabic language and the worship of Islam transcended regional concerns. Fortunately, he also found time to write, and his *Muqaddimah* and *Universal History* rank amongst the finest works to be produced in Arab history.

Ibn Khaldun was descended from a Spanish Arab family based in Seville that came to North Africa as refugees fleeing the onslaught of the Christian reconquest of the Iberian Peninsula. As a young man, he worked in the courts of Tunis and Morocco. Eventually he sailed for Spain, where, in 1364, he led a Muslim mission to negotiate a peace treaty with the ruthless Castilian king, Pedro the Cruel. His reward was an estate in Granada, the last Muslim kingdom in Spain, where he lived with his family. In the climate of the time, enemies were all too easy to make, and Ibn Khaldun was forced to abandon Granada for his personal safety and spent the next few years restlessly traveling around North Africa and Spain, working in various posts including that of prime minister in Algeria.

Before long, concerns for his personal safety forced him to move further afield, and having arranged to make a pilgrimage to Mecca, he stopped en route in Cairo in 1382. He was greatly impressed by what he saw. Writing of the city's splendor and wealth he was moved to quote the words of a former teacher who had declared: "What one sees in dreams surpasses reality, but all that one could dream of Cairo falls short of the truth."

For Ibn Khaldun, the Egyptian capital was also a wondrous oasis of learning. North Africa and Muslim Spain, he declared, had fallen into ruin, yet Egypt, whose thousands of years of unbroken tradition as a flourishing center of learning, in recent times reinforced by the Ayyubids and the Mamluks, served as a beacon that attracted students and scholars from Morocco to Iraq and beyond.

As was befitting of a man of his caliber, Ibn Khaldun began to teach at the famed al-Azhar Mosque, whilst also finding time to continue writing. Barquq, the sultan, who had summoned Ibn Khaldun on his arrival, soon promoted him to the prestigious post of Grand Qadi (or Chief Justice) of the Malikites, one of the four schools of Sunnism. It was a job in which he distinguished himself, reforming and routing out the corruption that was endemic in the legal system. The post exposed him to the intrigues of his enemies, however, and during his life he was forced to step down on no less than five occasions, only to be re-elected each time.

Ibn Khaldun had not intended to live in his adopted country alone. He sent for his family in 1384 to join him in Cairo, but tragedy struck. The entire family was drowned as their ship was wrecked approaching the port of Alexandria. Devastated, Ibn Khaldun yearned for a quieter life and, in 1387, finally made the pilgrimage to Mecca. On his return, he was chosen to head Egypt's most important Sufi convent. Yet before long, he was back in the limelight once again as Chief Justice.

In 1400, Ibn Khaldun's diplomatic skills were put to good use by the Mamluk government in the wake of a resurgence of Mongol power. Tamerlane, the Great Khan of Central Asia, had launched a major offensive westwards, taking Baghdad before marching onto Damascus, in Mamluk Syria, and laying siege to it. The Mongol conqueror had a fearsome reputation, slaughtering the inhabitants of the cities he captured and making pyramids of their skulls.

Ibn Khaldun was one of a number of notables who were chosen to accompany Barquq's ten-year-old successor, Nasir Faraj, to Damascus in order to negotiate a treaty. Ibn Khaldun, who had to be lowered over the walls of the city by rope, played an important part in its subsequent surrender and it was at this time that he got to see the Great Khan. At the meeting, he took the opportunity to show Tamerlane what he had written about him in his *Universal History*. The Mongol chief was apparently so delighted, that he took the opportunity to offer his own suggestions and opinions.

It was first-hand experience such as this, combined with a good knowledge of history, that put Ibn Khaldun in good stead as a fine historian. Yet it was his scientific approach to the subject, as demonstrated in the *Muqaddimah* (or *Introduction*) to his *Universal History,* that sealed his reputation as an extraordinary figure in the Muslim world. Begun in 1375, during a period of uncharacteristic seclusion in a castle in the present-day region of Algeria, the work brings together a wide variety of topics, including philosophy, religion, politics, economics, and even language to elaborate his theory of world history. When it came to geography, Ibn Khaldun's knowledge, like that of his Muslim contemporaries, was far superior to his European medieval counterparts.

His work, which he hoped might shed light on what factors contributed to the rise and fall of civilizations, has been hailed as the first comprehensive critical study of history, and one that pre-dated modern sociology by hundreds of years. Ibn Khaldun's genius as a writer and teacher earned him enormous respect from his peers, and he is generally credited with reviving historical writing in Egypt.

On March 17, 1406, while still in his sixth term as Chief Justice, Ibn Khaldun died at at the age of 74. His body was laid to rest in a Sufi cemetery in Cairo.

Arabian Nights in Mamluk Cairo

Mamluk Cairo also became the adopted home to what in the Western world is one of the most famous works of Arabic literature—the *Arabian Nights*, also known as *The Thousand and One Nights*. Frowned on by serious writers of the Arab world, these immensely popular folk stories began as a collection of Persian tales that were translated into Arabic in the early years of the Abbasid caliphate, sometime in the late 8th century. Originally the stories told of a sultan who was so outraged by his wife's infidelity that he decided to take a fresh wife every night and have her strangled in the morning. That was until he met the beautiful and shrewd princess Shahrazad (known in the West as Sheherazade), who kept him amused with her entertaining stories over a period of a thousand and one nights. The sultan was so captivated by Shahrazad in the end, that he spared her life.

Over the course of several centuries these tales were handed down orally, embellished and given a distinctive Arabic flavor. They gradually filtered into Egypt during the 11th century and Egyptians themselves began to adapt the stories to their own times, adding many of their own in the process. According to legend, it was the sultan's son who first entered the Great Pyramid of Khufu in Giza in search of a huge emerald.

The stories came to be known in Arabic as *Alf Layla wa Layl* (literally "A Thousand Nights and a Night"), but although the title suggests differently, there was never, in fact, a comprehensive collection of stories that amounted to that number.

The Fall of the Mamluks

With the ascendancy of the Burgi Mamluks, Egypt's fortunes began to worsen markedly. Political upheavals were compounded by a terrible outbreak, in the mid-14th century, of the Black Death: a horrific and highly contagious disease in which victims were struck first by boils, followed by prolonged bouts of vomiting blood and then, mercifully, death, usually within three days. The disease, which also reaked havoc in across Europe, wiped out around a third of the population of Cairo in the space of two years, and for many centuries to come, fresh outbreaks and epidemics of the plague would bring further misery and grief. On top of this, the Egyptians were creaking under the strain of extremely high taxes imposed by the ever greedier Mamluks. That Egypt did not collapse altogether was down to the fact that no group dared challenge the might of the Mamluks. Similarly, the Mamluks faced few serious challenges from overseas—their successful earlier campaigns had seen to that.

The Burgis were also somewhat unruly compared to the Bahris. Unlike the previous period in which the sultans were more or less chosen along the hereditary principle, now any prospective candidates for the sultanate had to use all their guile and influence to get elected by their peers. Furthermore, a new trend began of recruiting adult Circassian slaves. Unlike their young counterparts, these older slaves were less inclined to accept authority unquestioningly—a fact that contributed further to the growing instability of the regime.

Ultimately, the Mamluks' undoing came from their stubborn refusal to keep up with the times. After more than 250 years, they had successfully managed to use their military skills to keep themselves in power. First and foremost cavalrymen, they had certainly proved themselves to be amongst the finest of their age, but they had only a limited knowledge of the most modern weapons of war—firearms and artillery. Furthermore, they were loath to use them and even going so far as to dismiss guns as a cowardly choice of weapon. When they finally found themselves confronted by the might of the expanding Ottoman Empire, not surprisingly, they proved to be no match for its well-equipped and trained army.

The death blow finally came in 1516, after the Ottomans defeated the Mamluks at the Battle of Marj Dabiq in Syria. The Mamluks were slaughtered before they could even engage the enemy. The following year, in January 1517, the Ottomans entered Cairo and executed the sultan—the Mamluks could do little but accept the authority of the new invaders, but they were by no means finished.

THE OTTOMANS AND MUHAMMAD ALI

The Ottomans

Egypt was deprived of its Syrian territories in 1517, and became little more than an outpost of the Muslim Ottoman Empire. Despite attaining a great deal of independence in later years, it was formally to remain an Ottoman province until 1914. The Ottoman overlords were descended from nomadic Turkish tribes that had gradually moved from Central Asia to the region of present-day Turkey, eventually conquering the thousand-year-old Christian Byzantine Empire to which Egypt had belonged prior to the Arab conquest. After conquering Constantinople (Istanbul) in 1453, the Ottomans went on to amass a vast empire that, at its peak, included Greece, Serbia, Bulgaria, Syria, Arabia, North Africa, and, of course, Egypt.

The crescent and star were used as a symbol of both Islam and the Ottoman Empire.

The Ottomans wasted no time in capitalizing on Egypt's ability to produce foods such as grain, rice, and sugar, and on its potential as a rich source of taxes. Yet, for all intents and purposes, very little actually changed. As long as the Ottomans, who were too bogged down in wars in Europe and Persia to give Egypt their full attention, continued to receive what was due to them, they cared little about the details of the running of the country. Indeed, it was much more convenient to secure the allegiance of the Mamluks and have them keep order— in theory under the watchful eye of

Ottoman governors backed by a garrison of the Ottoman elite guard known as the Janissaries. Yet the governors, who were drawn from the bureaucratic ranks in Istanbul and appointed for one year only, proved inexperienced and mostly ineffectual. As a result, the Mamluk leaders, who now went by the Turkish title of *bey* meaning "lord", continued to effectively hold sway over the region.

Living up to their reputation, the Mamluks proved to be something of a handful. As the fortunes of the Ottoman Empire began to decline, so too did its hold over Egypt. Under Ali Bey, who ruled from 1760 to 1772, the Mamluks almost managed to reestablish absolute rule over the country. Ali Bey had ceased sending tribute to the Ottomans and had even begun to mint his own coins before the Ottomans finally managed to regain control. By the end of the 18th century, Egypt was in a state of near anarchy, severely weakened by years of civil war and incompetent leadership. In 1798, it thus found itself the unwitting victim of France's ambitious imperial policy, which would profoundly alter the course of Egyptian history.

The French Occupation

On July 1, 1798, a large French force, commanded by Napoleon Bonaparte, landed on Egyptian soil and stormed into Alexandria. Although Napoleon had invaded on the pretext of liberating the Egyptian people from the excesses of the Mamluks, the real objective was to turn Egypt into a French colony and further France's interests by blocking British access to India and the East.

The French arrived with high hopes for their intended colony. Accompanying their large army was what could best be described as a cultural battalion, comprising 167 eminent scholars, scientists and artists whose assignment was to investigate and record the country's past and present. The fruit of their labor was to be one of the most in-depth works ever published on Egypt, a 24-volume publication entitled *La Description de l'Égypte*, published between 1809 and 1813. It created such a stir in Europe that soon there was a continent-wide craze for all things Egyptian. Items such as clothing, furniture, and pottery were decorated with hieroglyphs, pyramids, sphinxes and other motifs.

Meanwhile, in a proclamation announced in Arabic, Napoleon attempted to convince Egyptian religious leaders and notables that the country had little to fear from the French. Declaring his deep respect for Islam, he announced that the French had come to put an end to years of misery caused by the Mamluks. As the baffled Egyptians were left to guess the true motives behind the invasion, Napoleon marched south to Cairo and defeated the outgunned Mamluks at the Battle of the Pyramids. By no means destroyed, the Mamluks withdrew to Upper Egypt and proceeded to wage an effective campaign of guerrilla warfare.

Now in control of the capital, the French began to set up their new administration. With a view to including Egyptians in the governing process, they invited the *Ulama* (the country's highly influential religious leaders) and other key figures to participate in central and regional councils. Yet, French dreams of a glorious role in Egypt were short-lived. The Egyptians failed to warm to their new governors, who expected them to pay for the upkeep of the French army.

Challenges from abroad similarly complicated their ambitions. On August 1, the French fleet was destroyed by the British Navy, commanded by Lord Horatio Nelson, at the Battle of the Nile. The following month, in Istanbul, the Ottoman sultan Selim III, who had actively been encouraging the Egyptians to get rid of Napoleon's troops, declared war on the French. Then, on October 21, there was a rebellion in Cairo. The French responded by throwing the might of their army at the Egyptians, quelling the

The Mediterranean port of Alexandria, where Napoleon began his occupation of Egypt.

immediate flames of revolt but merely igniting a new fire of resentment towards them.

The French were beginning to look truly beleaguered, but it was not the end of their misfortune. The following year, a military expedition into Palestine, which had gotten off to a good start, ended in utter disaster when the French laid siege to the city of Acre. For two months the besieged Ottoman garrison waited patiently as Napoleon's troops contracted malaria and dysentery, and dropped like flies around them. Napoleon, eager to get back to Europe, where he was destined for a somewhat brighter future as emperor, took the opportunity to sneak home to France. His unfortunate troops and scholars were left to their own fate in a hostile land, without a fleet to bring in supplies.

Napoleon's replacement was a general by the name of Jean-Baptiste Kléber. The commander attempted to negotiate his army's way out of Egypt, but to no avail. Fresh riots broke out, and French and Ottoman forces again clashed. Then on June 14, 1800, Kléber was assassinated by a young Syrian, Sulayman al-Habi. The French responded wrathfully, impaling the ill-fated assassin on a stake. Kléber's replacement, General Menou, found himself with few options. Even his conversion to Islam failed to endear him to the seething population of Cairo. It was all too late. Mercifully, the final blow came in September 1801, when a joint British-Ottoman force finally ejected what was left of the French army from Egypt. In the ensuing power struggle, a ruthless Albanian leader by the name of Muhammad Ali seized the reins of power.

Muhammad Ali

Despite lasting a mere three years, the failed French project was a catalyst that made Egyptians aware of some of the social and technological advances that had been taking place in Europe. But it was Muhammad Ali who helped Egypt take its first major step out of the medieval world. Although he only learned to write in his late forties, and never learned to speak Arabic, a combination of intelligence, charm and ruthless ambition allowed him to become the unquestionable ruler of Egypt—in spite of the fact that it never officially ceased to be an Ottoman province. It was Muhammad Ali who put an end to the troublesome Mamluks, leaving him free to embark on a series of reforms to ensure himself a place in Egyptian history as the Father of Modern Egypt.

Muhammad Ali was born in 1769 in the Ottoman coastal town of Kavala (now in Greece). He was the son of a local military commander, but after his father's early death, he was brought up by the town's governor. When he was old enough, Muhammad Ali gained a grounding in the military skills he would need later in life by participating in patrols to capture bandits and to enforce tax collections for the governor. After a spell working in the tobacco trade, Muhammad Ali ended up as commander of contingent of Albanian mercenaries that had been ordered by the Ottoman Sultan to help the British bring an end to the French occupation of Egypt.

Muhammad Ali—The "Father of Modern Egypt."

Although Egypt was supposedly back under the rule of the Sultan after the defeat of the French, the country was drifting in a state of virtual anarchy. In Cairo, the traumatized population had reached the end of its tether. It turned hopefully towards Muhammad Ali, whose troops had revolted against the Ottomans, to restore order. His popularity was such that the Ottoman sultan was hardly in a position to object, and Muhammad Ali was made the new vizier of Egypt in 1805.

He did not disappoint his supporters and skillfully negotiated his way through the murky waters of Egyptian politics by playing powerful factions against each other. Moreover, when it was time to take direct action, he was demonstrated an unflinching ruthlessness that made him a formidable opponent.

The most serious challenge to Muhammad Ali's rule were the Mamluks, who continued to hold sway over the Egyptian countryside. In 1811, after a series of battles, he managed to bring them to heel. Yet, he wanted to be sure that the matter was settled once and for all. To this end, arranged a huge celebration in honor of his son, who was about to set off to fight the Wahhabis in Arabia, and invited 500 Mamluk chiefs to the reception. Little did they know of the fate that was in store for them.

After the festivities, as they were making their way through a narrow passage to leave the citadel, they were cut off from the rest of the guests. The gates ahead were blocked. Suddenly, from above, Muhammad Ali's men fired a hail of bullets, killing most of the surprised Mamluks on the spot. Those who managed to survive were either shot then and there, or taken away and beheaded at the feet of Muhammad Ali. According to one English witness, the Citadel "looked like a hideous slaughterhouse, newly deluged with the blood of victims, and overstrewn with a multitude of reeking carcasses." The Mamluk chiefs lay lifeless by their horses "still clenching their scimitars with the last despairing, yet desperate grasp of death." It was said that only one Mamluk managed to escape the carnage, and he did so by forcing his horse to jump from the high citadel walls.

Immediately after the massacre, troops were sent out to find and kill any remaining Mamluks left in the country. Within a year, the last of those that had been holding out in Upper Egypt suffered the same violent and bloody end. Muhammad Ali had now successfully removed every serious challenge to his rule. Despite his new domain technically being a vassal state of the Ottoman Empire, he was a law unto himself.

Muhammad Ali's vision for the future of Egypt focused on Europe, which he greatly admired for its technological superiority. Surrounding himself with European professionals, he oversaw a wide range of military, economic and social reforms.

With the help of his French advisers, he created an education system that ended the centuries-old monopoly of the Quranic

The courtyard of the Mosque of Muhammad Ali.

schools, or *madrasas*. The educational reforms, which included sending students to study abroad in Europe, opened a new channel through which current Western ideas could filter into the country. On the medical front, his French advisers were instrumental in the creation hospitals and a basic public health system. Measures to prevent the spread of disease included draining swamps and keeping streets free from rubbish.

Although Egypt failed in its attempt at industrialization, the economy boomed as a result of the cotton industry. It had received a major boost after the introduction of a new variety of cotton plant that thrived in the Egyptian climate. Other achievements included the introduction of gas streetlights in Cairo and steamers on the Nile.

Yet, Muhammad Ali was first and foremost a military man, and his army was naturally of vital concern. With the help of a French colonel, a convert to Islam who was known as Sulayman Pasha, he transformed and modernized the army and navy. At its peak, during the 1830s, the Egyptian Army had a quarter of a million men and was unrivaled in the Middle East—a fact that not surprisingly made the Ottoman Empire extremely nervous.

Bolstered by his military successes in Egypt, Muhammad Ali began to look further afield, harboring dreams of an empire that would enable him to dominate the major trade routes of the eastern Mediterranean. Aided by his son Ibrahim, a talented military commander, Ali's policy of territorial expansion brought him early gains in Sudan and Arabia.

With his conquest of Syria, in 1831, Muhammad Ali posed a direct military threat to the Ottoman empire. The following year, Ibrahim advanced westward and scored a major victory at Konya, in Anatolia (Turkey). For a moment it seemed that he was poised to take the Ottoman capital of Constantinople.

It was Europe that stepped in to save the sultan. Peace in Europe hung on the delicate network of alliances, and its leaders had little interest in seeing anything that might upset the balance of power. Accordingly, the European governments came to the conclusion that it was time to check the ambitions of the rebellious Ottoman pasha. Interceding on behalf of the Ottoman sultan, they forced Muhammad Ali to compromise. In the peace agreement that followed, Egypt was permitted to hold onto its territories in return for an annual payment of tribute.

Yet, it was not long before Muhammad Ali was flexing his military muscle again and inflicting further defeats on the Ottoman forces. Alarmed by the increasingly likely prospect of being drawn into open conflict with each other, the European powers made a concerted effort to end Egyptian expansionism once and for all. In 1841 Muhammad Ali was forced to the negotiating table and given no choice but to sign an agreement that left him shorn of his territorial acquisitions. With his wings clipped, he now had to content himself with Egypt and Sudan only, and with an army a fraction of the size it had been.

Muhammad Ali remained ruler of Egypt until 1848, when, suffering from ill health and repeated bouts of dementia, he was forced to hand over the reigns of power to his son Ibrahim. Yet Ibrahim died within a matter of weeks. The following year, on August 2, 1849, Muhammad Ali died at the age of 80. The task of ruling Egypt now fell to Ali's eldest grandson, Abbas I.

Egypt Under Muhammad Ali's Successors

None of Muhammad Ali's successors showed his natural flair for leadership. There were some important achievements under Abbas I, however, including the construction of the first railway line in Africa. Built by the British, the line ran from Alexandria to Cairo and was extended to the port of Suez shortly thereafter. It was no coincidence that the railway proved to be of great benefit to Britain, becoming a major link in its communication network with India.

Abbas I did not share Muhammad Ali's like of foreigners and did much to reverse his policies, expelling his grandfather's French advisors in the process. Yet his reign was to prove short-lived—after only five years in power, he was assassinated by two of his slaves in 1854. He was succeeded by his uncle Said (r. 1854-1863), who revived the policy of seeking the help of European advisors. However, courting the Europeans would ultimately lead the country into the clutches of powerful British and French interests, where it would remain for decades to come.

The man who would ultimately led the country down the path of ruin and foreign dependence was another of Muhammad Ali's grandsons, Ismail, whose wildly extravagant rule lasted from 1863 until 1879.

Ismail was the first of Egypt's new rulers to be known as *khedive*, meaning "sovereign"—a title that he secured at considerable expense from the Sultan of the Ottoman Empire. Like Muhammad Ali, Ismail had a soft spot for all things European and, once in power, attempted to revive the reforms started by his famous grandfather. Great strides were made in education. Primary schools were opened to children of all religions, with fees on a sliding scale depending on the families' ability to pay. By the 1870s, the number of students had risen from a mere 6,000 during Muhammad Ali's rule to approximately 90,000. Nor was education restricted to boys—in fact, about a third of those in school were girls.

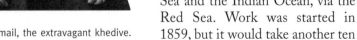

Ismail also oversaw reforms of Egypt's communications network, improving and constructing harbors, railways, roads, and bridges. Furthermore, with British assistance, he was instrumental in creating a highly efficient, modern postal system.

It was also Ismail's reign that saw the opening of the Suez Canal. Ismail's predecessor, Said, had granted the French a concession to build a canal to create a shipping route between the Mediterranean Sea and the Indian Ocean, via the Red Sea. Work was started in 1859, but it would take another ten

Ismail, the extravagant khedive.

years before it was finally completed.

Built by the French engineer Ferdinand de Lesseps, the canal, which was 100 miles long, was a remarkable achievement and a landmark event in world communication. It dramatically reduced the time taken to travel to India and the Far East, which previously required a lengthy journey around Africa by way of the Cape of Good Hope.

The Suez Canal was officially opened on November 18, 1869, amidst some of the greatest celebrations the country had ever seen. Ismail lavishly entertained the distinguished guests he invited from

Ferdinand de Lesseps, the French engineer who constructed the Suez Canal.

around the world, making sure they wanted for nothing. Indeed, if Ismail had dug even further into his pocket, the Statue of Liberty that stands in New York Harbor may well have ended up welcoming people to the Suez Canal. Inspired by the huge statues of Abu Simbel, Frederic Auguste Bartholdi originally intended to build the Statue of Liberty to commemorate the completion of the canal. Its flame was to symbolize Egypt at the cutting edge of progress, "carrying the light of Asia." However, the cost was such that even the extravagant and enthusiastic Ismail shied off the project. Undeterred, Bartholdi sold his idea elsewhere and finally got to see his statue built in the United States.

To pay for his grand schemes, Ismail borrowed vast sums from European financial institutions, bankrupting the country in the process. His financial mismanagement would soon lead him on a

Egyptian stamp commemorating the 100th anniversary of the Suez Canal.

collision course with his creditors, and to his downfall. The khedive commanded little respect from the populace. For the majority of Egyptians, Ismail's "Westernizing" reforms meant little, except the weight of heavier taxes piled on top of an already hard life—lived for the most part in abject poverty. It seemed that Ismail and his cronies were selling the country lock, stock, and barrel to foreigners in order to finance their own privileged and decadent lives. If proof were needed, it came when Ismail was forced to sell his 44 percent stake in the Suez Canal Company to the British in order to appease his creditors. As the loans and debts continued to mount, the French and British decided to intervene. In 1879, the Bureau of Public Debt was established to bring state finances under joint Anglo-French control and see that Ismail's creditors were paid.

The British and French also took the opportunity to get rid of the insolvent khedive. With little difficulty they pressured the Ottoman Sultan to replace him with his son, Muhammad Tewfik, on June 19, 1879. Without the support of his people, there was little recourse for Ismail, and he sailed into exile, never to return.

The Battle of Tel al-Kabir and the British Occupation

As Egypt lay foundering in economic ruin and sank ever further into the hands of foreign interests, a growing number of Egyptians began to express their dissatisfaction. This new voice was loudest in the army. While Egypt had relied heavily on imported soldiers such as the Mamluks until the beginning of the 19th century, this was no longer the case. As the army was reformed, it was staffed by men who were born and bred in the country and had a close affinity with the Egyptian population. This new element became increasingly sympathetic to growing nationalist sentiments—a development that the French and British were to watch carefully.

Soon a new movement, "Egypt for the Egyptians!" began to gain popular support in the country. It was inspired by a colonel in the Egyptian Army by the name of Ahmad Urabi. Urabi (born *c.* 1842) was amongst the first of the new native Egyptians to rise to the ranks of an officer. His outspoken criticism of the foreign control of state finances and the European-friendly khedive earned him a great deal of respect from the army, along with considerable popular support. In 1882, Urabi was appointed Minister of War. With his fellow officer Mahmud al-

Ahmad Urabi—his rebellion marked the ascendancy of Egyptian nationalism.

Barudi as prime minister, the renegade Egyptian posed a serious threat to the khedive and European interests.

The British and French were keen to nip the dangerous

movement in the bud and forced the government to resign. Yet Urabi was once again appointed Minister of War.

On July 11, 1882, after riots broke out in Alexandria, British ships heavily bombarded the city. As flames engulfed the city, the nervous khedive deserted his own government and sought refuge behind British guns. Urabi responded by issuing a declaration of war against Britain. The following month British troops were sent up the Suez Canal to face an ill-prepared army put together by Urabi. The two armies met on September 13, 1882, and the ensuing Battle of Tel al-Kabir was a lopsided bloodbath. Around 10,000 Egyptian soldiers were killed, while British fatalities amounted to less than 100.

Urabi was banished into exile, ensuring that he was no longer a direct threat to the British or the khedive. Years later he was allowed to return to Egypt after being pardoned by the khedive (then Abbas II), and died on September 21, 1911.

Despite its failure, Urabi's rebellion was a highly significant event in Egyptian history. As Britain's General Charles Gordon, famed for his last stand in Khartoum and an admirer of Urabi, noted: the Egyptians would never be such "obedient servants" again.

Egypt had now become of considerable strategic interest to Britain. However, the British government concluded that administering the country directly from London, as it did with its colonies, was unrealistic. Its empire was already stretched to its limits, and with growing rifts closer to home in Ireland, it would have been hard pressed to single-handedly control what was rapidly becoming an extremely resentful population. Instead it opted for indirect rule, bringing heavy pressure to bear on the "puppet" khedive and his government. The real authority in the land was, in fact, the British Consul-General who ensured that British interests were served. Thus Egypt never formally became part of the British Empire, but for many decades to come it would remain under its powerful influence and suffer the humiliation of a permanent British military force of occupation.

Britain also extended its military influence into Sudan. Despite a rebellion during the 1880s in which the Sudanese overthrew Egyptian forces, the country had initially been of little concern to Britain. This attitude changed, however, when the French began to extend their influence in West Africa. Little relishing the prospects of the French pushing into East Africa, Britain decided to send its forces into Sudan in the late 1890s. The British then established what in name was a joint Anglo-Egyptian rule, but in reality was run by them alone.

In addition to its strategic interest, there were economic benefits to be had from Egypt. Of prime interest was Egypt's ability to grow cheap cotton, which Britain needed for textile mills back in England. Accordingly, the British government began to maximize cotton production. At the same time, they levied considerable taxes that made Egyptian products unprofitable, ensuring that the domestic textile industry remained a lame duck.

When it came to the general administration of the country, Britain was eager to see that things ran smoothly with as few problems as possible. Keeping the elite rich and the poor adequately fed was the general policy, and by and large it worked. Yet there was no cause for complacency. The Battle of Tel al-Kabir had not silenced the voice of protest that had been raised against the British, and, as General Gordon had rightly predicted, there were more than a few "disobedient servants" who would do their best to bring it to a deafening crescendo.

Mustafa Kamil—The Voice of Egyptian Nationalism

Mustafa Kamil was amongst the growing number of Egyptians who refused to accept the British presence in Egypt. During his short life, he would become a driving force behind Egyptian nationalism and a persistent thorn in the side of the British government.

Kamil was born in 1874, the son of a native Egyptian army officer. From an early age he took a strong interest in history, and while still only a schoolchild displayed a surprising talent for making speeches. It was a skill that he would continue to develop and perfect, enabling him to convey his message with captivating eloquence.

While still a law student, Kamil became highly active in the nationalist cause. His commitment attracted the attention of the khedive Abbas II, who subsequently became his mentor. The young Swiss-educated khedive saw in him an opportunity to use the nationalist movement to help him secure his own dreams of independence from the British. (The latter made sure, under threat of "early retirement," that he did precisely what they required of him.)

Kamil was sent to France at the expense of the khedive, where he obtained a second degree in law, but where he also spent his time delivering speeches and writing articles in an attempt to get European support for his cause. Having found little success, Kamil returned to Egypt in 1894, and subsequently launched a campaign of demonstrations and strikes, supported by a loyal following of students who shared his vision of a British-free Egypt. Central to Kamil's demands were the evacuation of British troops from Egyptian soil and the drafting of a new constitution.

After gaining a great deal of experience writing for major Egyptian newspapers such as *Al-Ahram* (one of the country's best known papers today), he founded a paper in 1900 that was to become the mouthpiece for the nationalist movement—*Al-Liwa*. Two more newspapers followed in 1907—*The Egyptian Standard* (in English) and *L'Étandard Égyptienne* (in French). In addition to newspaper articles, he also wrote a number of books on the subject of conquest in history.

In 1906 a shocking and tragic incident occurred that did much to boost the popularity of Kamil's movement. A group of British soldiers had been out shooting pigeons near the village of Dinshaway, in the Delta region, when an argument broke out after villagers tried to get the soldiers leave. After scuffles, several of the villagers were injured and one soldier died—as it turned out, due to complications resulting from sunstroke. The British responded savagely. They rounded up a number of the villagers, put them on trial and and handed out the harshest of punishments. Four of the villagers were hanged, a number were imprisoned, including two for life, and several others were flogged. To make matters worse, the hangings and floggings were carried out in front of horrified family members and villagers who were forced to look on.

Kamil was quick to denounce the British government, and he was by no means alone. The brutality of the incident struck a deep chord in Egyptians from all walks of life, even in those who had British sympathies. It added fuel to the fire of what was until then a smoldering opposition to British rule. Even the British government had to concede that it had gone too far. Lord Cromer, the Consul-General, was forced to resign and the villagers who had been imprisoned were pardoned.

Kamil was struck down by tuberculosis and died in 1908 at the tragically young age of 34. However, his achievements as the leader of the nationalist movement lived on and provided a solid foundation for the Egyptian independence movement.

EGYPT IN THE 20TH CENTURY

World War I

I n 1914, after World War I broke out in Europe, the Ottoman Empire fatefully allied itself with Germany and the Austro-Hungarian Empire. The khedive Abbas II was immediately deposed by the British on account of his well-known pro-Ottoman sympathies and prevented from returning from Constantinople, where he had been on a visit. Britain then declared Egypt a protectorate and imposed martial law. Abbas's 60-year-old uncle, Hussein Kamil, was installed as the new head of Egypt. To make sure there was no confusion that the country had severed its ties with the Ottoman Empire, he was given the title of sultan, until then reserved exclusively by the Ottoman ruler.

Anti-British sentiment remained high during the course of the war, and there were increasing expectations that it would be followed by Egyptian independence—especially now that the country had been cut loose from the Ottomans. It was a time of hardship for most Egyptians, especially the poor. An enormous strain was placed on the country's food supplies, which were bought up in large quantities by the Britain to feed the huge number of troops stationed in the region. With food shortages leading to double pre-war prices, the poor struggled especially hard just to keep themselves from starving. Furthermore, the commandeering of some 20,000 peasants into British labor corps, where many would perish from disease, did little but increase resentment and further fuel the nationalist cause.

As the world conflict drew to a close towards the end of 1918, the British High Commissioner of Egypt received a visit by three

Egyptian politicians. Led by an extremely popular politician by the name of Saad Zaghlul (a lawyer by profession), they had come to demand independence and to be allowed to travel to London to put forward their case. Their request was refused outright. Undeterred, they announced their intention to send a delegation (*wafd* in Arabic) to the peace conference in Paris to present their argument there. Further British refusals sparked off waves of nationalist unrest throughout the country. In March 1919, Zaghlul was arrested by the British authorities and exiled to the Mediterranean island of Malta. The result was explosive. Anti-British sentiment erupted into widespread protests, strikes, and violent attacks on British citizens, including murder. The country languished in a state of paralysis as public transport came to a standstill and people stayed away from work.

Although the British soon managed to bring the situation under control, it had become clear that they would not be able to keep the lid on such feverish nationalist sentiment indefinitely. In an about-turn, the British government released Zaghlul and allowed him to go on to Paris and London. It was a fruitless mission, however, and a frustrated Zaghlul returned to Egypt in 1921.

The British continued to resist the inevitable for a while longer. Eventually, further riots and violence in the wake of the re-arrest and deportation of Zaghlul brought them to the conclusion that the protectorate was no longer viable. Without consulting the Egyptians, Britain declared Egypt an independent state on February 28, 1922.

An Unsatisfactory Independence

It seemed that independence had finally arrived, yet it was not exactly what the Egyptians had hoped for. The British were not readily going to relinquish the power they had over a country they considered to be of such strategic importance. Accordingly, independence had been granted on certain conditions that came to be known as the "Four Reserved Points." These were Britain's rights to safeguard its imperial communications in Egypt; to defend the country against foreign attack; to defend minorities and foreign interests; and to control Sudan. Given the circumstances, it was an offer the Egyptians could hardly refuse.

In 1923, a constitution was drafted by a National Assembly, and Egypt officially became a parliamentary monarchy. Fuad I, one of Ismail's sons who had become sultan after the death of Hussein in 1917, now took the title of king. A bicameral parliamentary system was established that consisted of a Chamber of Deputies and a Senate. Members of the former were elected by the adult male population, while two-thirds of those in the latter were appointed by the king.

In January 1924, Egypt celebrated its first general election. The

King Fuad I.

clear winner was Zaghlul's Wafd Party, which took its name from the delegation that he had led several years earlier. Zaghlul, who had been released the previous year and whose popularity was greater than ever, was now country's new prime minister, but attempting to govern the country would prove anything but straightforward.

Politics in the country became a three-way tug of war between the King, the Wafd, and the British government. Fuad I took advantage of the considerable powers granted to him under the constitution, and engaged in a personal crusade to frustrate the parliamentary process in order to serve his own ends. Indeed, thanks to his interference, intrigues and talent for playing the British and Wafd against each other, no elected parliament ever lasted its full term. For their part, the British exerted a great deal of influence through the High Commisioner and other officials who occupied key security posts in the government.

One of Zaghlul's main priorities was to see a decisive end to the British occupation of Egypt. This he believed would be possible by negotiating a treaty between the two countries. Furthermore, he was keen to fulfill the Wafdist dream of forcing the British to relinquish control of Sudan and then incorporating the territory into Egypt.

Zaghlul would never see his goals realized, and was soon overwhelmed by events beyond his control. On November 19, 1924, extremists with links to the Wafd Party assassinated Sir Lee Stack, the commander of the Egyptian army and Governor General of Sudan. The British government was furious. The High Commisioner, General Allenby, responded with a thinly veiled threat.

Allenby, a friend of Stack who was appropriately dubbed the "Bull," demanded that the government apologize and pay a fine of 500,000 Egyptian pounds. Furthermore, he insisted that Egypt withdraw its military personnel from Sudan—a gratuitous demand that clearly had nothing to do with the matter and merely demonstrated Allenby's bullying methods.

Insulted and outraged, Zaghlul rejected the ultimatum and promptly resigned. Allenby did not escape either. His handling of the affair had courted a great deal of displeasure at home and he was forced to resign. Despite continuing to lead the Wafd, Zaghlul's career was effectively over. He died a few years later in 1927, remaining as popular as ever until the end. His body was laid to rest in a huge granite tomb that still stands in Cairo.

Meanwhile, the three-way struggle continued. Little could be decided upon. King Fuad I worked hard at limiting the power and popularity of the Wafd and suspended the constitution, replacing Zaghlul's successor, Mustafa al-Nahhas, with Ismail Sidqi. Fuad I then forced through a new constitution that further strengthened his powers and allowed him to rule by decree. Between 1930 and 1933, Sidqi, backed by the king, imposed a hard-line rule over Egypt.

However, under continual pressure from the Wafd and the British, Fuad I found his position increasingly untenable. In April 1935, he was forced to restore the 1923 constitution. One year later he died and was succeeded by his son and successor.

With Faruq still too young to rule directly, the Wafd government seized the moment. Headed once again by al-Nahhas, it quickly negotiated a deal with the British government. On August 26, 1936, the Anglo-Egyptian Treaty was signed. This agreement replaced the "Four Reserved Points" and offered Britain a 20-year guarantee to protect the canal and other strategic zones in the event of war. Although it formally ended the British occupation of Egypt, it was a far from perfect settlement since British troops would not in fact be required to abandon the region until Egypt had proven its ability to defend itself.

At the age of 16, Faruq ascended the throne, yet little changed. Like Cleopatra so many years before him, the new king was the first in his line to be able to address his subjects in their own language. Like Cleopatra too, he was to preside over the end of his dynasty. But there the similarity ended. While the flamboyant young king paid lip service to nationalist ideals, he would never show the strength of character required to lead the country and challenge the British. He also found himself incapable of accommodating his government and, by December 1937, al-Nahhas was out once more and new elections brought in a disastrous result for the Wafd.

Umm Kulthum—Voice of the Arab World

Despite the disappointments and frustrations of its recent history, Egyptian society had by no means descended into gloom. Indeed, Cairo had blossomed into a vibrant cosmopolitan cultural center for artists, writers, and thinkers from all over the Arab world. Egypt itself produced its most enduring stars—such as the legendary singer Umm Kulthum.

Umm Kulthum was born to a poor rural family in 1904. She grew up in an extremely religious and musicial environment. Her father, Sheikh Ibrahim, was the *imam* of the village mosque and earned money from reciting from the Quran and singing spiritual songs at wedding ceremonies, funerals and other important occasions. While she was still a child, Umm Kulthum began to sing with her father, and before long it became apparent that she had a fine voice. Quick to recognize his daughter's talents, her father took her with him on his travels around the Delta region. Her father was not altogether comfortable singing with his daughter in public, however, and to ease his embarrassment he even had her dress in boy's clothes.

Encouraged by those around her, Umm Kulthum made the bold decision to move to Cairo at the age of twenty-two. There she underwent rigorous training to sing on stage, setting aside the simple style she had developed over the course of years with her father and embracing the popular romantic and modern songs that were performed with a backing group of accomplished musicians.

This was a time when Egypt was still reeling from the anti-British revolts that had exploded in 1919 and still coming to grips with its new-found independence. In Cairo, Umm Kulthum began to mix in exciting social circles, meeting important people who would shape her future career and the way she perceived

سيدة الغناءالعربى
أم كلثوم

Umm Kulthum

herself and her country. It was here, that she met the poet Ahmad Rami, who was to write many of the songs she sang. By the end of 1920s Umm Kulthum had risen to the top of her profession, and from the 1930s onwards no other singer in Egypt rivaled her.

With the creation of the Egyptian National Radio station in 1934, Umm Kulthum's career took on a new dimension. For the first time, she was able to bring her music into the people around the country who would never have had the opportunity to go to a theatre. It was a far cry from the days when she had traveled from village to village in order to perform her songs. The new relationship was to prove enduring and she would continue to woo radio, and later television, audiences for the rest of her career.

During the 1940s, Umm Kulthum began increasingly to turn towards a more indigenous style of music, which endeared her immensely to the rural population of which she was once a part.

When in her forties, Umm Kulthum began to suffer from the recurring bouts of ill health that would trouble her for the rest of her life. It was also a time in which she suffered one of the great disappointments of her life. Umm Kulthum was no stranger to the royal court, where she had sung for King Faruq, and there one of his uncles, Sharif Sabri Pasha, had asked her to marry him. Yet, despite the respect with which she was held in the country, her humble background was deemed by the royal family to be unsuitable and the matter was closed.

Perhaps not born of royalty, Umm Kulthum was nevertheless accorded the status of a queen by the Egyptians. But her fame was not restricted to her native country. During the 1960s, long after the unpopular royal family had been toppled, she was welcomed as an Egyptian stateswoman whenever she went abroad to give concerts and promote her country. She continued to sing up until 1973, when her ill-health finally got the better of her and forced her to stop. Two years, later, on February 3, 1975, she died in a hospital in Cairo. Outside, the media from around the Arab world had been camped out to keep their viewers and listeners with up-to-the-minute news on the condition of the beloved singer.

Her funeral was a momentous occasion. Millions of mourners packed the streets of Cairo to say farewell. In the charged emotional atmosphere, things did not go quite according to plan. The huge crowd seized her body and carried it off to her favorite mosque. After prayers of mourning were said, the *imam* of the mosque eventually persuaded them to take it to where she was to be buried.

Umm Kulthum's popularity did not end with her death—she continues to to hold a special place in the hearts of many and to this day is considered by many to be the Voice of the Arab world.

Egypt in World War II

In 1939, the European powers plunged the world into another major conflict. Although Egypt would become the arena of one of the most decisive battles of the war, that of El Alamein, and played a pivotal role in providing the British with supplies, there was very little overall support for Britain. Following a policy of non-belligerency, Egypt was, nevertheless, careful to fulfill its obligations set out under the Anglo-Egyptian Treaty of 1936. It declared a State of Siege and put its ports, aerodromes, and railways at the disposition of Britain. The Egyptian Army itself was limited to the defense of Egyptian territory, which by and large meant helping to protect the Suez Canal from mines and cities from air raids. The number of Egyptian troops killed during the war was estimated to be around 200.

The policy of non-belligerency was seen by the British as something of an advantage. It provided them with a relatively stable base to conduct its military operations. It was through the port of Suez that the Americans channeled vital supplies for the huge force engaged in the Battle of El Alamein. Cairo also became a hive of activity during the conflict, with Allied politicians, generals and hundreds of thousands of troops passing through.

The loss of Egypt was a scenario the British would not entertain. The British prime minister, Winston Churchill, declared that his country would defend the country to the end. When the Germans threatened to bomb Cairo, the British government issued a chilling warning to respond in kind. It vowed that Germany's Axis ally, Italy, could expect its capital to be systematically bombed for as long as the war lasted. The threat against Rome worked and Cairo was spared the destruction suffered by so many cities during the war. Alexandria was less lucky and was subjected to bombardment that caused a number of casualties.

The war caused serious disruption of everyday life in Egypt. Rampant inflation and serious shortages of basic foodstuffs hit the poor especially hard. The Black Market boomed. Too much cotton was being grown and not enough cereals. Attempting to compensate by reducing the area of land under cotton production made the government highly unpopular with cotton farmers and helped to boost the opposition. Some Egyptians pointed the finger of blame at the British and the huge amounts food needed to support its army. Although Britain denied it was pillaging the country since it also importing huge quantities of food, the accusation was, nevertheless, readily exploited by political agitators with Axis sympathies.

The ambiguity shown by the Egyptians towards the war reflected the views of a people that saw themselves as citizens of country that already had a struggle on its hands—against the British, not the Germans. Therefore, wherever their sympathies lay, there was one common thread—the desire for independence from Britain.

The Wafd Party headed by al-Nahhas, for example, opted to cooperate with the British, convinced that Britain would acknowledge its debt by ending its occupation of Egypt at the end of the war. Some, such as the Saadist Party (a breakaway faction of the Wafd), went so far as to argue in favor of declaring war on Germany. They were keenly aware that this would ensure Egypt a part in the reward of the peace process. Many opposed this, including the king, since after Germany invaded France many believed that Britain might well lose the war. If this were the case, Germany might well be the liberator of Egypt from British occupation.

There were also many individuals and organizations whose sympathies lay squarely with the Axis powers. Amongst the more extreme of anti-British groups was the Muslim Brotherhood.

Founded in 1928 by Hassan al-Banna, it was a highly organized movement that had at its disposal a variety of publications. Its aim was (as it still is today) to impose a strict form of Islamic government on Egypt. The Muslim Brotherhood was vociferously anti-British and therefore played an important role in the struggle for independence. For those who belonged to more moderate nationalist groups and envisaged a secular Egypt, the Muslim Brotherhood made for a somewhat disturbing ally.

King Faruq.

British concerns over Egyptian ministers harboring sympathies for the Axis powers twice led it to intervene in the country's politics and force a change of government. On the second occasion, in February 1942, British tanks were dispatched to the gates of the royal palace to help persuade King Faruq to allow the pro-British Wafd to form a government. The crisis led to bitter recriminations. Egyptians poured scorn on their king for his display of subservience, and the Wafd, now too closely identified with the British, similarly lost a great deal of credibility which it would never regain.

The Post-War Upheavals

The victory of the Allies over the Germans came in 1945, but despite demands by the Wafd that they now leave Egypt, the British failed to react. It was the last straw. The Egyptians, their patience utterly exhausted, took matters into their own hands. When the Wafd won a landslide victory in new elections, its government, headed by al-Nahhas, declared the 1936 Anglo-Egyptian Treaty void. Furthermore, the intense anger of the Muslim Brotherhood, muted for the duration of the war, erupted to the surface and manifested itself in a wave of anti-British demonstrations, riots and strikes.

By early 1952, the situation in Egypt had become explosive. In the Suez Canal Zone matters came to a head after a newspaper published a reward of a thousand Egyptian pounds for anyone who would kill the British general in charge of the Canal. The general in question, Sir George Erskine, responded by cracking down on Egyptian police who were suspected of having dealings with anti-British terrorist organizations operating in the region. Soon events got out of hand, resulting in a full-scale siege of a police barracks. Facing strong resistance, British forces stormed the building with the aid of tanks, leaving 50 Egyptians dead and many others wounded.

The event shocked and outraged the Egyptians, provoking a huge demonstration against the British and King Faruq, whose popularity had reached an all-time low. Soon Cairo was literally on fire as furious mobs went on the rampage. In an attempt to bring the situation under control, the king declared martial law and dismissed the Wafd government. It was too late. The fate of the country now lay outside the hands the politicians and in those of the Egyptian army.

The Birth of the New Republic

On the night of July 22, 1952, a group of disillusioned military officers belonging to a clandestine organization known as the "Free Officers," rose up in arms against the government and, without having to fire a shot, they rapidly seized control of the country's key institutions. King Faruq was forced to abdicate in favor of his infant son Fuad II, and, on July 26, he sailed away to exile in Italy on board his royal yacht. He died in Rome in 1965.

The Free Officers formed a committee, known as the Revolutionary Command Council (RCC), and appointed a general by the name of Muhammad Naguib as prime minister. In 1953, the monarchy was formally abolished. Egypt was now a republic and Naguib was duly named the country's new leader. It was a landmark event in Egypt's history—the first time since the pharaonic era, more than 2,000 years before, that the country was ruled by a native Egyptian.

Yet Naguib's leadership was illusory. The real leader behind the revolution was an extremely charismatic young Egyptian officer named Abdel Gamal Nasser, who had assumed the role of deputy Prime Minister and Minister of the Interior.

Nasser was born on January 15, 1918 in Alexandria, the son of a post office manager. While still only a schoolboy, he took part in anti-British street protests and later remembered that whenever he saw a plane in the sky he would shout: *"Ya 'Azeez, ya 'Azeez. dahiya takhud al-Ingleez."* (Almighty God, may a calamity befall the English!) At the age of seventeen, Nasser's forehead was grazed by a police bullet at a huge pro-Wafd demonstration in Cairo, leaving him with a scar that he carried with him for the rest of his life. Graduating from the Royal Military Academy, Nasser went on to a career in the army, where he would rise spectacularly to fame. In time he would become greatest hero of the 20th-century Arab world, idolized for his defiant stand against the domination of the West and his campaign for pan-Arab unity.

Under the new regime, there was no room for opposition—the press was heavily censored and political parties outlawed. Only the Muslim Brotherhood escaped the ban, until it was implicated in a plot to take Nasser's life in October 1954. Nasser responded with a vengeance, outlawing the organization, executing some of its leaders and throwing several thousand other suspects into prison.

That same year, Nasser came to the decision that Naguib, who had openly enjoyed the support of the Muslim Brotherhood, had served his purpose. Accusing him of conspiring against the state, Nasser had him placed under house arrest. Nasser was then free to set about consolidating his power as acting head of state. In January 1956, a new constitution was drafted, and Egypt was

Abdel Gamal Nasser—champion of the Arab World.

declared a democratic republic. After seeking the population's approval by means of a referendum, Nasser formally assumed the role of president, armed with a wide range of constitutionally-granted powers.

Despite Nasser's ruthlessness towards the opposition, he was to embark on a series of policies that would seal his popularity at home and abroad. His program of reforms to improve social conditions for the poor of the countryside, where there were glaring inequalities, gained him a groundswell of support. In fact, the process had started as early as September 1952, when the new regime had enacted reforms to bring an end to the deeply conservative social order in the country by breaking up large estates and redistributing land to the peasants. The result was not, in fact, the end of rural inequality, but the creation of a new wealthy class of peasants who began to monopolize economic and political power. With a rising population and a lack of employment, many began to seek a better life in urban areas, adding to a growing problem of overcrowding in the cities.

When it came to foreign policy, Nasser found himself the undisputed leader of the Arab world, at least for the first part of his rule. A committed pan-Arabist who believed that Egypt was the natural leader of the Arab and Muslim world, Nasser spoke out loudly against foreign, particularly British, interference in Arab affairs. It was little surprise that his major priority had been to end the British occupation of the Suez Canal Zone. In July 1954, after intense and frustrating negotiations, Britain had finally agreed to leave the zone. The British government insisted on an important clause in the agreement. It stipulated that should any of the Arab League member states be attacked, it would be free to re-deploy its forces to protect the waterway.

Two years later, in June 1956, the last British soldier left Egyptian soil. It was an enormously significant event—not since the last century had Egypt been free of British forces. Having successfully negotiated his treaty with the British, Nasser was free to turn his attention to the intensely bitter conflict that had been raging in the Middle East over the creation of the state of Israel.

The Roots of the Egyptian-Israeli Conflict

For the duration of his premiership, Nasser would pit his wits against his arch-enemy, Israel. From the start, the relationship between Egypt and Israel was a stormy one, leading to a series of conflicts, the causes of which are complex and lie within the wider history of the region.

The key issue was the strong and enduring Arab opposition to Zionism, a movement that believed in the right of the homeless Jewish nation to establish a permanent state in Palestine and that began to gain widespread popularity in Europe during the 1890s. In 1917, in a document known as the Balfour Declaration, the British government expressed its support for the idea, on the condition that it not infringe on the rights of the non-Jewish population of Palestine. At the time, the Jewish community there counted for around only seven percent of the population, the rest being Arabic-speaking Muslims and Christians. Britain's support for Zionism was extremely significant, since, in the aftermath of the World War I, the British government officially assumed control of the former Ottoman province of Palestine.

During the first decade of its rule, Britain had to contend with a succession of anti-Zionist riots, but matters got decidedly worse during the mid-1930s. The rise of Hitler and his Nazi Party in Germany in 1933 had put into motion the terrible campaign of persecution that would eventually lead to the systematic murder of around six million Jews in Europe.

Barred from entering other European countries, Jewish immigrants began to flood into Palestine. Tensions mounted and, in 1936, the Arabs staged a full-scale revolt. In an attempt to solve the problem, Britain announced a proposal to partition Palestine between the Arabs and Jews. The Arabs rejected the idea outright, leaving the British to struggle in vain to come up with a workable solution to the problem.

In the aftermath of World War II and the Holocaust, the flood of Jewish immigrants to Palestine turned into a torrent. The Arab world, spurred on by its opposition to a Jewish state and its need to foster unity amongst its ranks, created a new organization called the League of Arab States (or the Arab League). Established in Cairo, in 1945, its earlier members were Arab countries in the

Middle East, including Egypt, Syria and Transjordan (from 1949 onwards called Jordan), but it later expanded to include many other Arab states.

With tension between the Arabs and Jews at a breaking point, the British government finally threw in the towel. On February 18, 1947, Britain's Foreign Secretary, Ernest Bevin made his country's position clear by announcing: "His Majesty's government have of themselves no power to award the country either to the Arabs or the Jews, or even to partition it between them." In the opinion of the British authorities, there was only one course open, and that was to let the newly-established United Nations find an answer.

The newly formed international organization was hardly in an enviable position. The Arabs rejected the partition of Palestine, favoring instead the creation of a single state with the guarantee of equal representation of Muslim, Jewish and Christian communities alike. On the other hand, the Jews favored the creation of two separate states. The U.N. opted for partition. But by now it hardly mattered anyway. The region was rapidly becoming engulfed in a spiral of violence committed by terrorists on both sides, and there seemed little hope of implementing the U.N. plan in a peaceful manner. Instead, the Jews took matters into their own hands.

The Arab-Israeli Conflict

On the afternoon of May 14, 1948, the Jewish leader in Palestine, David Ben-Gurion, declared a new Jewish independent state called Israel. The answer from the Arab world was swift. In their eyes, the Jews had illegitimately seized Arab territories and alienated Palestinians from their rightful homeland.

The following morning, Egyptian fighter planes flew over the city of Tel Aviv. Around the newly created Jewish state, neighboring Arab countries—Egypt, Syria, Lebanon, Jordan and Iraq—began massing their forces.

Despite being swift to respond, the Arab forces were anything but prepared and even lacked any clear consensus as to whether war was the proper way forward. In Egypt there were many, including the incumbent prime minister, who questioned the wisdom of risking a costly war with Israel when the main priority was to get the British out of their own country once and for all. Despite these reservations, Egypt closed ranks with its fellow Arab League members and went to war.

With its contribution of around 15,000 troops, Egypt fielded the largest force. Like the majority of its Arab allies, however, it lacked adequate supplies, equipment, and experience. Once the war was fully under way, the Israelis rapidly gained the upper hand. On June 10, a U.N.-sponsored ceasefire was declared and, despite a fresh outbreak hostilities, the outcome had already been decided. Along with its allies, Egypt had to accept the failure of their venture and swallow the fact that Israel, a country they refused to officially recognize, was now in possession of around a third more territory than that provided for under the U.N. partition plan—including one-half of Jerusalem.

An immediate effect of the conflict was the creation of hundreds of thousands of Arab Palestinian refugees. Fleeing into the Gaza Strip and neighboring Arab countries, they turned desperately to the U.N. for humanitarian aid. As the Palestinians fled, Jewish immigrants flooded into Israel, doubling the Jewish population of the country over the next three years.

Relations between Egypt and Israel had gotten off to the worst possible start, and for the three decades the two countries would remain in a state of virtual open warfare. This tense relationship came to dominate the political agenda in Egypt. Nasser was himself a veteran of the Arab-Israeli war, and, upon coming to power, he became acutely aware that his credibility as a leader of the Arab world would hinge on how well he handled Israel.

Meanwhile, a number of events took place that worsened an already desperate climate. In October 1953, the Israeli village of Yahoud was attacked, leaving an Israeli mother and her two children dead. In retaliation, the Israelis launched an all-out attack on the village of Qibya in Jordan, killing 69 people. Denounced as unjustifiably heavy-handed, the attack provoked outrage throughout the Arab world.

The following the year, on July 14, undercover Israeli agents were caught after placing bombs in U.S. and British buildings in Cairo and Alexandria. The intention had been to make it look as though it were the work of Arabs. By creating tensions between Egypt and the West, the Israelis hoped to scuttle plans to remove British troops from the Canal Zone, which served as a valuable buffer between Israel and Egypt. They further hoped to ruin Egypt's chances of receiving military aid from the United States. The plan backfired miserably when the perpetrators were caught and subsequently tried by the Egyptians. Two were executed and the others imprisoned. The event served little more than to destroy the last vestige of hope for an understanding between the two countries.

Events came to a head in February 1955, after yet another tit-for-tat round of hostilities. In response to the discovery of an Egyptian spy plot against the Israelis, and a separate incident in which an Israeli was attacked and killed, Israel launched a retaliatory attack on a military base in the Egyptian-held territory of Gaza in Palestine, which left 39 Egyptian soldiers dead. As was the case in the attack on Qibya, a year and a half before, it caused an outcry in the Arab world, which saw the taking of 39 lives for one Israeli life as far too harsh.

Image of Nasser in a gesture of solidarity for Palestine.

Nasser's Defiance of the West

It was at this point that Nasser resolved to find weapons to boost Egypt's fighting potential. Hoping to gain them from the Britain or the United States, he was frustrated by the condition that they not be used against Israel and that Egypt should join the West in an anti-Communist alliance. Undeterred, Nasser turned to the Communist bloc and purchased his arms from Czechoslovakia instead. In the tense climate of the Cold War, the West took an extremely dim view of Nasser's defiance. But from the Arab world, it brought rapturous applause. Nasser had shown the world that an Arab country could make its own decisions and choose its own destiny. Like Saladin against the Crusaders, Nasser was seen as a new champion who had stood up to the West and would lead the Arabs to victory in Palestine by defeating the Israelis.

Nasser's star had risen, and the following year he pulled off the most dramatic and popular moves of his career. It came in July 1956, after the United States, annoyed by Nasser's drift away from the West, withdrew its support for an ambitious project to construct a huge new dam at Aswan in the south of Egypt. The dam was the linchpin in a massive program to boost the Egyptian economy. By controlling the waters of the Nile, it would protect the country from the worst effects of drought, increase the area of land under cultivation, and provide a massive boost to industry by generating enormous supplies of hydroelectricity.

Nasser was furious at the U.S. withdrawal of support and took the bold step of nationalizing the Suez Canal Company. He further rejected any suggestion that the canal be managed by a new international body. The canal was Egyptian, and the revenue it earned—which, as Nasser was quick to point out, made the proposed U.S. aid for the dam project look ridiculous in comparison—would be ploughed back into Egypt to fund the construction of the dam.

Nasser's Aswan Dam was eventually constructed, taking 30,000 workers ten years to complete. Finished in 1972, it now measures more than 12,000 feet long (two and one-quarter miles) along the top and stands 360 feet high. At its base it is 3,200 feet thick and 130 feet at its top. The huge body of water it created, named Lake Nasser, is an astonishing 300 miles long, with an average width of over 6 miles, and extends well into neighboring Sudan.

The flooding of such a great area of land inevitably posed serious problems for local inhabitants and around 100,000 people had to be resettled. Another cause for concern was the fate of major archeological sites, especially the temples of Abu Simbel, which would be lost forever under the waters of the artificial lake.

A woman carries a load against the backdrop of the Aswan Dam.

At the behest of the Egyptian and Sudanese government, a huge rescue appeal was launched with the support of UNESCO. In what was to prove an unparalleled feat of modern engineering, two temples built by Ramses II were moved block by block and rebuilt on higher land. Many other temples in the region were similarly saved from destruction.

Britain and France Challenge Nasser

The nationalization of the canal came as a huge shock for the British and French, who had come to look on the canal as almost their own private concern. Now in the twilight of its days as an empire, Britain was especially indignant at the loss of control of the waterway, which was a major route for oil supplies from the Arab Gulf and still considered an imperial lifeline.

The French too were annoyed at the Egyptians over the loss of the canal that they had built and managed. To add to this, they were smarting over Egypt's involvement in financing an independence movement in France's colony of Algeria. The bottom line was that neither power trusted Nasser, and believed (quite wrongly as it turned out) that the Egyptians would be incapable of running the canal. Joining forces against Nasser, they immediately laid plans to retake it by force and bring down his regime.

The ruse they dreamed up involved giving themselves a supposedly clear-cut justification to invade Egypt. In what was to prove to be a political debacle, the two countries secretly asked Israel to invade Egypt. The Israelis were only too happy to oblige and, on October 29, 1956, they marched their army into Sinai. The British and French governments then deviously issued an ultimatum calling on both Egypt and Israel to withdraw their troops from the immediate vicinity of the canal. Since only Egyptian troops were actually in the exclusion zone at the time, the British and French had given themselves a reason to attack Nasser's forces under the guise of protecting the canal. Wasting no time, they landed a force of paratroopers who seized control of the waterway. During the course of the operation, Egypt's airforce was destroyed while still on the ground. Meanwhile, the Israelis had successfully advanced through Sinai and taken control of the entire peninsula.

From a military point of view, the operation was a success. However, politically it was a disaster that backfired in a most spectacular fashion. That two Western powers might invade a country in such an underhanded way caused widespread outrage and was condemned outright by the United Nations. The British and French might possibly have weathered the storm of international criticism had it not been for the fact that the United States was also dumbstruck by the recklessness of its supposed allies, who had acted without consultation. Accordingly, it joined in the chorus of U.N. disapproval.

The ill thought-out fiasco ended in utter humiliation for the British and French. Isolated and without the backing of the United States, there was little alternative but to back down. Yet there was one winner—President Nasser. His standing rocketed to almost mythical proportions amongst the Arabs.

Early in 1957, Britain and France evacuated Egypt, and ships that had been scuttled by the Egyptians to block the canal were cleared by the U.N. The Egyptians continued a ban against Israeli ships using the waterway, but let them use the Gulf of Aqaba as a route south into the Red Sea. For the next ten years, the U.N. policed the uneasy borders between the two countries. In the meantime Nasser turned his attention to his pan-Arab dreams.

A Brief Pan-Arab Experiment

In 1958, Egypt and Syria made the bold move of uniting to form a single state called the United Arab Republic, with Nasser as president. What at first appeared to be a landmark event in Arab unity turned out to be a short-lived and highly unpopular marriage, with the Syrians little disposed to taking orders from Egypt. The inevitable divorce came in 1962.

Another Arab commitment was failing to bring about the desired results. In 1962, hot on the heels of the failed Syrian experiment, Nasser found what he believed would be a good opportunity to strike a blow at the reactionary forces of the Arab world, which he held to be responsible for preventing Arab progress. Accusing them of being stooges of the Western imperialist powers, Nasser made the decision to send Egyptian troops to Yemen to support a revolution that had broken out to topple the royal elite and establish a republic.

Despite hopes that there would be a speedy conclusion to the conflict, it dragged on for several years and proved extremely costly both in terms of lives and money. Nasser himself referred to it as his "Vietnam." Failed attempts to find a solution to the war through the Arab League only served to highlight deep divisions in the Arab world and did little to maintain Nasser's reputation as its hero.

As the 1960s progressed, Nasser also became increasingly sensitive to criticisms from the Arab world that he had gone soft on the Israelis and lacked the courage to stand up to them. It was no longer Egypt that was taking the lead in challenging Israel but Syria, which had begun to mount limited but sustained guerrilla warfare against the Israelis.

The Six-Day War

In May 1967, as tension mounted on the Israeli-Syrian border, Nasser felt compelled to make a show of defiance towards Israel. After ordering the removal of the U.N. peacekeeping force that was stationed along the Egyptian-Israeli border, on May 22, he announced the closure of the Gulf of Aqaba to Israeli ships, thus preventing them access to the Red Sea. To the Israelis he declared defiantly: "The Jews threaten war and we are ready. Welcome!"

The Israelis accepted Nasser's challenge on June 5, 1967, launching an all out-out attack that caught the Egyptians completely unawares. In a perfectly executed operation, Israeli planes destroyed Egypt's airforce on the ground. Without vital air cover, Nasser's army had no chance against Israeli forces that had stormed into the Sinai Peninsula, and had little choice but to retreat.

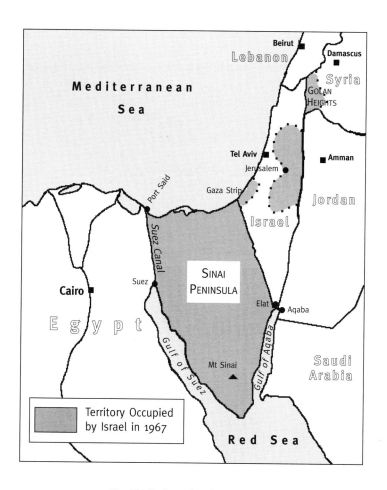

The Middle East after the 1967 War.

In the onslaught that followed, thousands of Egyptian soldiers were killed and wounded. Meanwhile, Jordan and Syria, who had launched attacks against Israel in support of Egypt, were similarly defeated. It was a massive and humiliating defeat for Egypt and its allies.

The war was a bitter personal blow to Nasser, the man who during the 1950s had commanded such respect throughout the Arab world. In a matter of a few days, Israel had taken control of the whole of the Sinai Peninsula and brought the front line between the two countries up to the Suez Canal. In addition to this, Israel seized and occupied substantial territories in the neighboring countries of Jordan and Syria—the West Bank, including the whole of Jerusalem, and the Golan Heights. Following the Six-Day War, as it became known, the United Nations passed a resolution calling for an Israeli withdrawal. It was not until 1970, however, after a two-year war of attrition, that a comprehensive cease-fire was finally brokered.

On September 28, 1970, President Nasser died unexpectedly after suffering a heart attack at the age of 52. Despite being a highly controversial figure until the end, Nasser's death came as a profound shock to the Arab world. Still a hero in the eyes of many, he was given a spectacular funeral. In all, some four million mourners attended his funeral (the largest the world had seen, according to *The Guinness Book of Records*), including leaders and top-level politicians from around the world. Such was the stature of the Egyptian statesman that even Nasser's detractors—Britain, France and the United States—felt compelled to send representatives.

Sadat—The Long Road Towards Peace

Nasser was succeeded by his vice-president, Anwar al-Sadat, a companion of many years who many believed would be no more than a minor and transitory leader. They could not have been further from the truth.

Muhammad Anwar al-Sadat was born in a Delta village on December 25, 1918, the son of a clerk and a Sudanese woman. From his humble beginnings, Sadat eventually went on to graduate from the Military Academy in Cairo in 1938.

The young Sadat actively supported Misr al-Fatat (a nationalist youth movement with pro-Fascist tendencies) and the Muslim Brotherhood. During World War II, he established links with German agents and was subsequently expelled from the Army and imprisoned. After the war, he was back in prison on charges of conspiracy to assassinate al-Nahhas and Amin Uthman, a pro-British Wafdist minister, but was acquitted in 1948. Sadat rejoined the Army and together with Nasser played a major role in the "Free Officers" coup to oust King Faruq. In 1969, Nasser appointed him vice-president, but he showed little overall signs of ambition.

Anwar al-Sadat.

In fact, Sadat owed his presidency to the fact that no one had ever believed he posed a threat to the power structure erected by Nasser. Prior to becoming president, he had even humbly acknowledged that he would not pretend to be a new Nasser, but would simply do as he was told by the regime and ensure that its directives were carried out. Yet appearances were deceptive. Sadat was no mere puppet, and charting his own course, he came to significantly alter the course of Egyptian history—confounding the Arab world in the process.

Whereas Nasser had turned to the Soviet Union for military support and turned his back on the West, Sadat courted the West and reestablished diplomatic links with the United States that had been severed in the aftermath of the 1967 War. In July 1972, he ordered the expulsion of some 20,000 Soviet military advisors. Furthermore, Sadat was not concerned with playing the pan-Arabist statesman, but chose to put national interests back at the top of the agenda. In 1971 he laid to rest the last vestiges of Nasser's dreams for a greater Arab state—no longer would the country be known as the United Arab Republic, but instead as the Arab Republic of Egypt.

Sadat's overriding concern was to get back Sinai, which had been lost to Israel in the 1967 War. Initially, he hoped that by distancing himself from the Soviet Union he would be in a better position to secure U.S. support to negotiate the return of the land. His overtures fell on deaf ears, however, and he became increasingly convinced that the only way to get Israel to the negotiating table was by threatening it militarily. In 1973, Sadat cast aside his doubts and put into action his plan of war, which he spent a year carefully nurturing.

The Yom Kippur War

The Egyptian leader's plan, conceived in October 1972, was to cross over to the east bank of the Suez Canal, breaking through the Israeli defenses and occupying a strip of territory stretching just over six miles into Sinai. He believed this to be a realistic objective that would create enough of a stir to force Israel and the international community to pay attention to Egypt's demands. As part of the operation, he persuaded the Syrians to agree to launch a simultaneous attack on northern Israel with an aim to splitting the Israeli army. Yet Sadat knew his plan would only succeed if he took the Israelis by surprise. To this end he spent many months mobilizing his forces repeatedly and then sending them home after a few days. The continual military movement was a source of great puzzlement to the Israelis and, at one point, when it seemed that an attack was surely imminent, the Israelis responded by mobilizing too. It turned out to be yet another false alarm and when the Egyptians sent their troops home, the Israelis followed suit.

The mobilization of Israel's army was a huge undertaking. Its reserves were made up of huge numbers of the civilian workforce, and for as long as they were in uniform, the country's economy lay in a state of paralysis. It was little surprise then that the Israeli government was reluctant to go through the expense and stress of having to mobilize its army unless they were absolutely convinced that Egypt intended to attack. Sadat knew this too, and his enemy was playing right into his hands.

On October 6, 1973, at precisely two o'clock in the afternoon, after a year of patiently waiting, Sadat's forces began their attack. Having got it wrong before, and convinced that the Egyptians would never choose to fight during the month of Ramadan, the Israeli government failed to respond. Furthermore, since it was the major Jewish festival of Yom Kippur, most Israelis were in the middle of celebrations and had no idea their country had just been attacked by Egypt and Syria. They were completely caught off guard.

Sadat's plan was initially a complete success. His troops managed to cross the canal and seize control over the territory as they had planned. Emboldened by his success, however, Sadat became too ambitious and decided push on into the Sinai Desert. It was a fateful decision. The Israelis had now managed to gather themselves and launched a counter-attack that left the over-stretched Egyptian forces on the defensive. To the north of Israel, the Syrians too had been pushed back, with the Israelis reestablishing control over the Golan Heights and marching to within 25 miles of the Syrian capital, Damascus.

When it looked as if the Israelis were on the point of inflicting a crushing defeat on Egypt, the United States brought intense pressure to bear on the Israeli government and made them agree to a ceasefire. A key concern was that if the Soviet Union decided to get involved and took sides against Israel, the conflict might escalate into a superpower confrontation. Sadat's impulsiveness may have brought him military defeat, but he had managed, nevertheless, to achieve his initial goal—that of forcing the Israelis to the negotiating table.

Peace with Israel

In 1977, after two years of stalled negotiations, President Sadat made the historic decision to go in person to Israel to initiate top-level talks with the Israeli government. The following year he teamed up with the Israeli prime minister, Menachem Begin, to negotiate a comprehensive peace treaty between the two countries. This became known as the Camp David Accords, so named after the U.S. presidential retreat in Maryland where negotiations took place. Under the new agreement, signed by the two leaders in Washington on March 26, 1979, Israel agreed to hand back Sinai to Egypt and to work towards Palestinian autonomy in the West Bank and Gaza Strip. After years spent at war with each other, the two countries had finally agreed to peace.

The effort won Sadat and Begin the 1978 Nobel Peace Prize. Sinai was subsequently returned to Egypt, but coming up with a workable solution to the issue of Palestinian autonomy proved elusive. Indeed, as the 21st century dawned, the search for a peaceful solution to the problem remained as urgent and desperate as ever.

Although Sadat's reputation had risen to the loftiest of heights in the West, it could hardly have sunk any lower in the Arab world. The Arab community rewarded the Egyptians by suspending them from the Arab League. Its headquarters were forthwith transferred from Cairo to Tunisia.

This was not the only alarming development. Another was the effect of the peace deal on the growing Islamic fundamentalist movements which had now joined in a deafening chorus of disapproval. Islamic movements in general had been gaining a great deal of popularity during the 1970s, taking advantage of a thaw in the political climate that saw the lifting of press censorship in 1974 and the legalization of parties in 1977.

That was not to say there was much in the way of democracy in Egypt. In order to gain official recognition, opposition parties had to fulfill a wide range of requirements and the few that were successful were prevented from gaining all but a few seats in parliament—it was always the pro-government National Democratic Party that would win the lion's share of votes.

More political freedom meant greater criticism, especially after the peace with Israel, and Sadat's response was to tighten the reins with increasingly repressive measures. In 1980, he even went so far as to enact a "Law of Shame," which made it an illegal and punishable offense to make speeches or engage in activities that attacked his policies.

As Egyptian society became more politicized, tensions began to mount between Muslims and Coptic Christians, erupting in serious riots between the two sides in Cairo and Alexandria.

Finally, in September 1981, as violent clashes continued, an angry Sadat launched a major crackdown on a number of oppositional groups, both Muslim and Christian. Hundreds of their members were arrested and their publications banned. Furthermore, the government assumed tight control over the activities of mosques and other religious institutions in the country For good measure, Sadat arrested and ousted the head of the Coptic church, Pope Shenouda III, replacing him with a council of bishops.

Pope Shenouda III.

In the midst of the worsening political climate, Sadat paid the ultimate price for incurring the displeasure of his Muslim opponents. On October 6, 1981, the president, surrounded by a large entourage, was reviewing a military parade commemorating the eighth anniversary of the Yom Kippur War. As all eyes were turned to a jet display overhead, a group of four men, armed with machine-guns and grenades, jumped out of a truck that was taking part in the parade and rushed over to where Sadat was seated. Within a matter of seconds, the stand was engulfed in a hail of bullets and smoke. Sadat was hit repeatedly at close range and died shortly afterwards. In the aftermath it emerged that the assassins and their accomplices, who were subsequently caught and executed, belonged to a Muslim fundamentalist organization whose aim was to establish an Islamic state in Egypt. The attack was a clear demonstration of the lengths to which religious extremists would go to pursue their goals. It was left to Sadat's successor, Hosni Mubarak, to tackle them head-on.

Naguib Mahfouz—Chronicler of Cairo

Violence at the hands of extremists was by no means limited to politicians such as Sadat. Expressing personal opinions on sensitive subjects such as religion and politics was a risky business and it almost brought a premature end to the life of one of Egypt's greatest writers, Naguib Mahfouz.

Nobel Prize winner Naguib Mahfouz is one of the few modern Arabic novelists to achieve a truly international status. His reputation as an outstanding author has earned him the respect not only of his own country, but also of the Arab world.

Mahfouz was in born in Al-Jamaliyya, an old quarter of Cairo, on December 11, 1911. He was the son of a middle-class civil servant and the youngest of seven children. Mahfouz was rather a quiet child and spent a good deal of his time reading. He studied philosophy at Cairo University and graduated in 1934. After a brief spell as a journalist, he embarked on a career as a civil servant—a line of work he felt would afford him more time to work on his novels.

Naguib Mahfouz.

In 1939, his first novel, *The Games of Fate*, was published. It marked the beginning of a prolific output that includes some 30 novels, in addition to numerous short stories. Of special interest during his early career is *The Struggle of Thebes*, a novel influenced by the historical romances of Walter Scott and based on ancient Egyptian history. In it, he draws a parallel between the struggle by the Egyptians to expel the foreign Hyksos and the modern British occupation of Egypt.

Amongst Mahfouz's most famous works is his *Cairo Trilogy* published in the 1950s. Named after alleys in the Al-Jamaliyya district of Cairo, the three books—*The Palace Walk*, *Palace of Desire*, and *Sugar Street*—trace the lives of a cast of fascinating characters through three generations that stretch from World War I to the 1950s. In them, the author offers the reader a wonderful and insightful glimpse into social and religious attitudes of the time.

However, Mahfouz's exploration of his own society courted a great deal of controversy in the Arab world. This was especially the case with his book The Children of Gebelawi, published in 1959. In it he portrayed everyday Egyptians in the role of religious characters, including Moses, Jesus and Muhammad. Mahfouz was barraged with accusations of blasphemy on account of his treatment of Islam, and his book was subsequently banned in many Arab countries.

Mahfouz's outspoken support for the peace treaty with Israel earned him further criticism and censorship in the Arab world. Speaking of the period during which Sadat was assassinated, the author likened the situation to a "woman facing a difficult pregnancy," a time during which he explained "we must rebuild the social classes in Egypt, and change the way things were during Nasser's time."

In 1988, Mahfouz was awarded the Nobel Prize for Literature for his wonderful novel, *Midaq Alley*, which explores the frictions between modern and traditional Egypt. He was the first Arab novelist ever to win the prize. The Swedish Academy of Letters hailed his novels as works that formed an "Arabic narrative art" that applied to all mankind. Mahfouz's writing has won him numerous other awards, including the Egyptian State Prize on two occasions. He was also made an honorary member of the American Academy and Institute of Letters and Arts in 1992 and, three years later, was awarded an honorary doctorate by the American University of Cairo.

Still the subject of great controversy, Mahfouz narrowly escaped death in October 1994, after being stabbed in the neck outside his home in Cairo by a Muslim fundamentalist who had taken offense at his work.

Although much weakened by the attack, Mahfouz was still actively writing in his 90s and his dedication to his art is best summed by his own declaration that: "If the urge to write should ever leave me, I want that day to be my last."

Mubarak—Continuing Sadat's Legacy

On October 14, 1981, eight days after Sadat's assassination, his vice president Muhammad Hosni Mubarak was sworn in as president. He had been nominated by the People's Assembly and received 98 percent of the votes in a national referendum.

Under Mubarak, Egypt entered a period of relative stability. Relations with the rest of the Arab world began to thaw after the years of isolation brought about by Sadat's policies. In 1989 Egypt was finally welcomed back into the Arab League and, the following year, its headquarters were finally transferred back to Cairo.

A portrait of Muhammad Hosni Mubarak, taken from a popular banner.

As well as actively supporting the Arab-Israeli peace process, and meeting with leaders on both sides, Mubarak also maintained Sadat's policy of friendship with its allies in the West, developing ever stronger military and financial ties. Indeed, Egypt proved to be an important player in the Gulf War in 1991, joining the U.S.-led Western coalition that helped to liberate Kuwait after it was invaded by Iraqi forces under Sadam Hussein.

During the conflict, Egypt committed more than 30,000 of its troops.

Religious fundamentalism remained a major challenge for Mubarak, and as Sadat had done before, the Egyptian government began a huge crackdown on members of religious fundamentalist organizations, arresting many hundreds of people in the process and declaring a period of marital law.

In an attempt to provide himself with clear popular backing for economic reforms and to counter the alarming popularity of the Islamic movements, whose ranks were swelling with increasing numbers of Egyptians who felt alienated from the political process, Mubarak hoped to able to introduce greater democracy. To this end, the Wafd party was allowed to reform and all political parties, with the exception of the Muslim Brotherhood, were free to participate in elections in 1984. Yet, the elections failed to satisfy expectations of greater representation. The government National

The skyline of Cairo.

Democratic Party (NDP) gained more than 85 percent of the seats. The Wafd for its part managed to win 57 seats.

During the mid-1980s, a fall in oil the country's oil revenues and mounting debts led to increasing economic worries. Islamic fundamentalism continued unabated into the 1990s, bringing yet more economic and social problems, as witnessed by a wave of terrorist attacks aimed at numerous targets: among them, government officials, Copts and foreign tourists. A particularly troublesome organization was the Islamic Group (*Gama'at Islamiya*), which had sworn to depose Mubarak and establish an Islamic government. It was this group that was behind a series of horrific attacks that resulted in the deaths of a number of foreign tourists and that shocked not only the outside world, but also left many Egyptians saddened. The attacks proved to be disastrous for the Egyptian economy for a time, as tourists shunned the country.

Burg al-Qahira (Tower of Cairo) — built in 1957,
it stands 157 meters high.

THE NEW MILLENNIUM

The new millennium has brought with it major challenges for the Egyptian nation. Some of the more pressing problems are especially related to the country's expanding population, which has put ever greater strain on the country's limited resources. Despite the terrorist attacks of the 1990s, which brought about a great deal of anguish and suffering, the country continues to enjoy political stability. Furthermore, it is easy to point to the tensions created by religious fundamentalism in Egypt, yet forget that overall it is a progressive country. Its longstanding reputation for ethnic and religious tolerance is still intact, while the women living within its borders enjoy some of the greatest freedoms in the Arab world.

Not so long ago, Egypt was desperately trying to break free from the influence of the British Empire—the last in a long line of foreign powers to dominate the country. Present-day Egypt, however, has put those days behind it and reestablished a new and friendly relationship with the West from a position of ever growing strength and confidence.

Egypt has always influenced and been influenced by the wider world, and its future as a major player on the international stage is certain. Its struggle to resolve the tensions between the modern and traditional forces of the country is one that concerns the international community at large, and its influence in North Africa and the volatile oil-producing Middle East cannot be underestimated. However far away lies a satisfactory and lasting solution to the confrontation between Israel and Palestine, Egypt will almost certainly take a lead role in ensuring a chance of enduring peace.

With its cosmopolitan and liberalizing tendencies, Egypt provides an natural gateway for the West to enter into a meaningful dialogue with the wider Arab world. Hopefully the opportunity will not be lost. For the Egyptians themselves, the greatest challenge is now the long and difficult road in the march towards what many see as its most pressing goal—to secure stable and lasting democracy.

CHRONOLOGY

3100 B.C.	Unification of Egypt
2700-2200	Old Kingdom
2220-2050	First Intermediate Period
2050-1750	Middle Kingdom
1750-1580	Second Intermediate Period; Hyksos invade
1580-1200	New Kingdom
1200-330	Third Intermediate Period and Late Dynastic Periods; Assyrian and Persian invasions
332	Alexander's conquest of Egypt
323-30	Greek Ptolemies
30 B.C.-639 A.D.	Roman and Byzantine rule
639	Arabic invasion and the introduction of Islam
661	Umayyads (ruled from Damascus, Syria)
750	Abbasids (ruled from Baghdad)
868-905	Tulunids
934-969	Abbasids; Ikshidids
969	Fatimid Dynasty
1169	Saladin becomes vizier of Egypt
1171-1250	Ayyubids
1250-1382	Bahri Mamluks
1382-1517	Burgi Mamluks
1517	Egypt becomes Ottoman province
1760-1772	Ali Bey establishes own rule in Egypt
1798	Napolean invades Egypt and establishes French rule
1801	France defeated and expelled from Egypt
1805	Muhammad Ali appointed vizier of Egypt
1811	Mamluk leaders massacred by Muhammad Ali
1849	Muhammad Ali dies
1849-54	Abbas I

1854-63	Said
1859	Construction of Suez Canal begins—opens in 1869
1863-79	Khedive Ismail
1879	Britain and France take control of Egyptian State finances; Ismail exiled
1879	Khedive Muhammad Tewfik
1882	Urabi's revolution and Battle of Tel al-Kabir; Britain begins occupation of Egypt
1892	Khedive Abbas II
1914	World War I—Egypt declared a protectorate; Khedive Abbas II deposed by British and Hussein Kamil made sultan as Egypt breaks with Ottoman Empire
1917	Fuad becomes sultan
1918	Zaghlul heads *wafd* to demand independence
1919	Mass uprising in protest against the British
1922	Britain grants Egypt conditional "independence"
1923	Constitutional Monarchy declared; Fuad made king
1924	Zaghlul resigns after assassination of General Stack
1936	Fuad dies; Faruq succeeds; Anglo-Egyptian Treaty signed
1939	World War II, Egypt declares policy of non-belligerency
1942	Britain forces Faruq to install pro-British Wafd government
1948	Arab-Israeli war; Egypt and allies defeated
1952	Faruq deposed
1953	Egypt declared a Republic
1956	Nasser made president—nationalizes Suez Canal; Britain and France invade Egypt but withdraw
1958	United Arab Republic (Egypt and Syria) created (dissolved in 1962)
1962	Egypt sends troops to fight civil war in Yemen
1967	Egypt defeated by Israel in Six-Day War
1970	Nasser dies; Sadat made president

Chronology

INDEX

Index

Index